Mystic Musings in Art and Poetry

Mystic Musings in Art and Poetry

Thematic Essays
From the International Conference
'Mysticism without Bounds'

Editor
Dr. Kurian Kachappilly, CMI

CWI

Christian World Imprints™

First Published in 2013 by

Christian World Imprints(TM)
Christian Publishing & Books from India
H-12 Bali Nagar, **New Delhi-110015**
info@christianworldimprints.com
www.ChristianWorldImprints.com
More at: www.kkagencies.co.in/sitemap
Phone: +91 11 25465925 Fax: +91 11 25173055

ISBN-13: 978-81-925121-1-2 ISBN-10: 81-925121-1-8

Cataloging in Publication Data—DK
[Courtesy: D.K. Agencies (P) Ltd. <docinfo@dkagencies.com>]

Mystic musings in art and poetry : thematic essays from
the International Conference 'Mysticism without Bounds' /
editor, Kurian Kachappilly.
p. cm.
Includes bibliographical references and index.
ISBN 9788192512112

1. Mysticism in art—Congresses. 2. Mysticism in literature—Congresses.
3. Mysticism and poetry—Congresses. I. Kachappilly, Kurian.

DDC 204.22 23

Printed at Chawla Offset Printers

Dedication
To

Blessed Kuriakose Elias Chavara
-a mystic and poet-
who has inspired many in their pursuit of wisdom;
"the Supreme Wisdom, which is devotion to God"

The Book

'Mysticism' is "the pursuit of communion with, identity with, or conscious awareness of an ultimate reality, divinity, spiritual truth, or God, through direct experience, intuition or insight." The International Conference "Mysticism without Bounds" makes an attempt to explore the "mystical consciousness" from different disciplines, like religions (Hinduism, Judaism, Christianity, Islam, Buddhism, Taoism, etc), sciences (biology, new physics, neuroscience, and logic), humanities (philosophy, theology, spirituality, psychology, etc.), and art forms (poetry, music, dance, visual arts and rituals).

Researches reveal that certain common grounds do exist among the various forms of consciousness, scattered among the world's religions, theologies, sciences, philosophies and art forms. The discovery of such points of convergence holds out the possibility of creating a 'new worldview', and this new world view can create an awareness of the essential 'unity' of humanity. Let these scholarly papers, presented from different domains of art and poetry, help the inquisitive readers to discover this essential unity, which is often conceived and interpreted in terms of 'God-experience' with its basis within non-phenomenal self, and a unity that promises the unity of all experiences within the phenomenal world.

The Editor

Dr. Kurian Kachappilly is the Professor of Philosophy and Religion at the DVK, Bangalore, India; and Associate Director, Research Centre, Christ University, Bangalore, India. He holds Master's Degrees in English Literature and Psychology, and a Licentiate and Doctorate in Philosophy from the Katholieke Universiteit Leuven, Belgium. He is a Visiting Fellow at the Bangalore University, Bangalore; Katholieke Universiteit Leuven (KUL), Belgium; Fakultät für Informatik & Wirtschaftsinformatik, Würzburg, Germany; the University of Santo Tomas, Manila, the Philippines; and other institutions.

He is the Executive Editor of *Tattva*, Journal of Philosophy, Christ University, Bangalore; a Member of the International Advisory Board, *Process Studies*, Claremont, USA; a Member of the Pontifical Organization, *Militia Christi*, and a Member of the Governing Board, International Process Network (IPN). Dr. Kachappilly is a prolific writer with several books and many scientific articles to his credit. Some of the books include *God of Love Revisited* (1998), *Between Partners* (1999), *Word of God Retold* (2001), *God of Love: A Neoclassical Inquiry* (2002), *God-Talk Reconstructed: An Introduction to Philosophy of God* (2006), *Process: Implications and Applications* (2006), etc. His major areas of research are 'Indian Roots of Process Philosophy', 'Whitehead and Philosophical Doctrines of Buddhism', 'Innovative Experiments in Pedagogy', 'Religion vis a vis Society', 'Inquiry into Religious Experience' and 'Corporate Social Responsibility'.

Contents

1

A Note from the Editor

Dr. Kurian Kachappilly, CMI
Christ University, India

'Mysticism' (from the Greek *mystikos*) is "the pursuit of communion with, identity with, or conscious awareness of an ultimate reality, divinity, spiritual truth, or God, through direct experience, intuition or insight."[1] In fact, there is no one single definition or common description of mysticism, for mysticism is a trans-cultural phenomenon, found in all different religions. Strictly speaking, mysticism is not to be connected with religions per se, for its scope is very wide, embracing all realms of human thought. Hence in "Mysticism without Bounds" (MwB2011) an attempt is made to explore the "mystical consciousness" from different disciplines, like religions (Hinduism, Judaism, Christianity, Islam, Buddhism, Taoism, etc), sciences (biology, new physics, neuroscience, and logic), humanities (philosophy, theology, spirituality, psychology, etc.), and art forms (poetry, music, dance, visual arts and rituals).

The MwB2011 was jointly organized by Christ University and the DVK, under the aegis of Dharmaram College, which was attended by over 320 delegates from thirty countries, like Australia, Belgium, Canada, China, Congo, Germany, Korea, Japan, Nigeria, Philippines, South Africa, Sweden, Thailand, UK and USA. There were about 200 Indian delegates from different universities, faculties, institutes and centres across the Indian Subcontinent. There were also representatives

[1] http://en.wikipedia.org/wiki/Mysticism

from various Indian Associations, like ACPI (Association of Christian Philosophers of India), BAP (Bangalore Academy of Philosophers), KPC (Kerala Philosophical Congress), and ILAAM (Indian Leuven Alumni Association Meeting). About 150 scholarly papers were presented in five parallel sessions, chaired by delegates, participants and invited guests, in addition to the key-note papers. Some of the highlights of the MwB2011 include (i) Inauguration by Rev. Jose Panthaplamthottiyil, (ii) Presidential Address by Swami Veda Bharati, (iii) Key-note papers by Dr. Bernard McGinn (USA), Dr. Paul Moyaert (Belgium), Dr. Peter Tyler (UK), Dr. Reimund Bieringer (Belgium), Dr. Una Agnew (Ireland) and Dr. Francis Vineeth (India).

May I place on record my heartfelt thanks and appreciation to all the delegates, presenters, participants, event partners, who have extended their wholehearted support toward the successful organization of the MwB2011, especially to all the heads of the institutions: Dr. Augustine Thottakara (Rector, Dharmaram College), Dr. Thomas C. Mathew (Vice Chancellor, Christ University) and Dr. Francis Thonippara (President, DVK); Dr. Lieven Boeve (Dean, Faculty of Theology, KUL, Belgium); Dr. Antoon Vandevelde (Dean, Institute of Philosophy, KUL, Belgium); and Dr. Annette Meuthrath (Asia Desk, Institute of Missiology Missio, Aachen, Germany). In a special way, I do acknowledge with thanks my great indebtedness to the administration and office-bearers of the Institute of Missiology Missio, Aachen, Germany, for their generous contribution and support toward the organization of the International Conference, 'Mysticism without Bounds' (MwB2011), from January 05-08, 2011.

Many art forms are not only ways for mystics to communicate what they are trying to teach, but they have also helped shape the minds and imaginations of the mystics. Poetry is an art form that has lent itself to reflection and contemplation on the nature of reality, human conditions and levels of consciousness. For mystics, poetry serves as one of the most powerful expressions of their inner experiences. At times mystics attain a state of consciousness that is beyond the usual awareness of humanity; but they find it hard to describe these levels of consciousness. However through poetry mystics try to give a glimpse of their moments of illumination. Poetry, as Colin Wilson argues, is "a contradiction of the habitual prison of daily life and shows the way to transcend the ordinary world through an act of intense attention-and-intention." The poet, like the mystic, is subject to sudden "peak experiences" when "everything we look upon is blessed" (*Poetry and Mysticism*, 1969). In the words of Santayana "Poetry raised to its highest power is then identical with religion grasped in its inmost truth; at their point of union both reach their utmost purity and beneficence, for then poetry loses its frivolity and ceases to demoralize, while religion surrenders its illusions and ceases to deceive" (*The Essential Santayana: Selected Writings*, 2009).

Like poetry, music, dance, visual arts and rituals have emerged as fascinating ways to connect the undifferentiated states of oneness, non-duality, and the differentiated states of diversity and multiplicity. Gerardus van der Leeuw, for instance, explains how music helps us overcome all boundaries: "Music leads into the depths of life, there where the boundaries flee away" (*Sacred and Profane Beauty*, 1963, 257). Similarly, art's function to represent reality as matter-spirit continuum, human icons as sacred stories, music as an agent of transcendence, poetry as symbolic and suggestive method of communication and communion with the divine, sacraments as ways of uniting humanity with God, and rituals as models of symbolic essentialism, are some of the major themes in the New Age Spirituality.

In the essay "Leonard Cohen's Poiesis: Toward the Unified Heart Where all Bounds Fade Away," Dr. Alexandra Pleshoyano explores the significance of Leonard Cohen's dual belonging, by addressing the following questions: How does he conciliate Judaism with Buddhism? How does the act of *poïesis* help Cohen to connect the undifferentiated states of oneness, and the differentiated states of multiplicity? Having presented Cohen's experience with Buddhism and Judaism, Dr. Pleshoyano argues how music, for example, can become a mystical means to overcome all differences; and she concludes by bringing forth the role of mysticism as a common ground favouring thereby the contemporary interfaith and intercultural dialogue.

Dr. Ignatius Bambang Sugiharto in his essay "Negative Memory, Art and the World Peace" dwells upon the dual role of art. Art, on the one hand, expresses the negativity, that is, the void, the chaos, or the spiritual blindness of the socio-cultural plight. But, on the other, it also serves as a diagnostic tool for identifying the disease; a process of intensifying and heightening our perceptual awareness of the crises; a necessary visualization of the critical interface between body, mind and soul. Thus Art, for Dr. Ignatius Bambang Sugiharto, renders palpable the ugliness, the meanness, the unbearableness of life, and this, in turn, will open the possibility to see what ultimately is more desirable, the deeper mystery of the soul, what we usually call 'peace'.

In "Confronting God 'As Such': Between Poetry and Phenomenology in the 'Mysticism' of Derrida," Dr. Colby Dickinson explores Derrida's rich reworking of the *as if* in order to arrive at the *as such*, given through the exploration of poets such as Wallace Stevens, Adrienne Rich and Paul Celan as well as the various mystical traditions which Derrida himself took up on occasion. By doing so, Dr. Dickinson hopes to show how Derrida's work ultimately points toward an encounter of the O/other *as such*, which is, in the end, the only real way to fully respect the encounter at all. In such a fashion, an ethics appears in the event of encounter, one that does not seek to reduce the singularity of the O/other's presence before us to a regulative ideal, but rather embraces what cannot be represented, bringing philosophy, politics and religion to the threshold of a mystical-ethical imperative.

In the paper, "Identifying the Mystical in Literature: Space versus Place in the Works of Willa Cather," Ms. Elisabeth Bayley explores the work of the American author Willa Cather and looks at the different ways her novels portray both one's literal space and culturally inscribed place as essential attributes to mystical experiences. By using Michel de Certeau's notion of space and place in the everyday experiences of life, Ms. Bayley examines Cather's fiction and the ways in which she situates different characters' experiences of the everyday life and yet how these experiences, though bound by both space and place, have the capacity to transcend them, thereby acquiring their 'mystical' attributes.

In "The moon won't use the door/only the window: Mystical Romance and the Construction of Voice in the Poems of Jelaludeen Rumi," Dr. Jayanthi Kalpally Puthiyaveetil traces the construction of the mystical voice in Rumi's poems and his encounter with Shams of Tabriz and the genealogy of its romance with the Divine. Sufi cult in Islam, to which Mewlana Jelaluddin Rumi belongs, focuses the concept of union with God by tapping in the innate knowledge within the individual: "[...] on the reparation of the heart and turning it away from all else but God". Rumi's poems, as Dr. Puthiyaveetil argues, celebrate the power of love and silence, while living in the present moment in the awareness: "Loving God is the only pleasure".

"Music and Mysticism: The Emergence of Musical Meaning" by Dr. Marlies de Munck is a praiseworthy attempt to highlight music's strong affinity with the mystical experience that has been systematically underplayed and even deliberately repressed by relegating music to the role of obedient servant of the Word. Taking into account music's historical roots, Dr. de Munck puts forward the hypothesis that the higher reality, the 'beyond' to which the musical tones originally helped to relate in ritual and magical practices, has been taken up entirely by the music itself. That is, music, as a perfect instrument, helps us open up our hearts and minds and to lead us to moments of self-transcendence and intimate communion with a 'higher' reality.

Dr. Sanchita Choudhury's article, "Bāuls, Mystic Minstrels of Bengal: Builders of a New Tomorrow in the Realm of Global Music," explores the living philosophy of Bāuls manifested in their songs and the conspicuous transformation of both their philosophy and music in the global era. Although some Bauls, she observes, are attempting to preserve the traditional form of Bāul music, a liberal infusion of musical elements of 'other' genres and the intrusion of intercultural elements of modern fusion music seem to have transformed century old traditional Bāul forms.

"Art and Mysticism: Space as an Aesthetic Predicate" is a scholarly presentation in which Dr. Sebastian Elavathingal investigates the relationship of art and mysticism to a dynamic and creative notion of "space." Art and Mysticism have a common interest: both are concerned about the spirit-matter dialectic and hence mediate between the physical and the metaphysical realms of reality. According to the author the new physics has brought in a new understanding of the physical world, which has changed the idea of the empty space into the idea of dynamic space of interrelatedness; and the new space consciousness is confirming the traditional, pre-modern understanding of space in rituals and classical art.

"Mysticism and Art: Beyond Abstraction and Empathy" by Dr. Stéphane Symons focuses on that type of experiences in which the universe *does not* resonate with our inner selves but nevertheless allows the limits of our ego's to be gradually dissolved in a way that is, rather than anxiety-provoking, consciousness-enhancing. Unlike the Western post-Enlightenment tradition, which seems to suggest that only when the outside world is felt to resonate in some way with our inner spirit that a genuine experience of mystical unity sets in (*Einfühlung* or empathy), these experiences are intimately connected with that part of our selves that belongs to the exterior world, our bodies, and is sharply distinguished from a purely rational insight about the unity of the universe (sublime) or from recognition of a spiritual content that is expressed in matter.

Finally, Ms. Winnie Jagadamma Panicker in her "Visualisation through Poetry: Concept of Spirituality and God in *The Prophet*," discusses how various visuals have been used in the poems and how the idea that God resides in every human being has been talked about by Kahlil Gibran. Visualization, for Panicker, is the way in which words transform into images in the mind of a person; and in poetry, the poet as well as the readers visualize the sequences while writing and reading. The poems that are taken to prove the point are from *The Prophet*: Religion, Prayer, Death, Freedom, Self-Knowledge, Good and Evil and Beauty.

Let these scholarly and challenging papers from different forms of art create an awareness among the inquisitive readers of the need of overcoming the 'bounds' of individuation and discovering the 'unity' of self, which the international conference 'Mysticism without Bounds' (MwB2011) aims at: "One who knows only the differentiated experience [...] comes to know an undifferentiated experience," the experience of "the primal self, *das Urselbst*" (Martin Buber, 1909). The unity of self is often conceived and interpreted in terms of 'God-experience' with its basis within non-phenomenal self, and a unity that promises the unity of all experiences within the phenomenal world.

2

Presidential Address

"Mysticism without Bounds"

Rev. Jose Panthaplamthottiyil, CMI
Vice Chancellor, Dharmaram Vidya Kshetram, India

1. Introduction

I am very happy and delighted to be here on this auspicious and inspiring occasion of this international seminar for serious study and research on the manifold dimensions of mysticism. At the very outset please allow me to congratulate the creative organizers of this seminar, an imaginative and innovative step in the field of researches. I am happier still that the seminar focuses on the interdisciplinary potentialities implied in the very nature and structure of mysticism. Mysticism, to my mind, is beyond the bounds of reason and steeped in human experience. At the very heart of mysticism there is an intimate interconnectedness, between the sacred and the secular, between the infinite and the finite, between the ultimate and the immediate. This inner interconnectedness between nature and reason is the root of the creative thought of interdisciplinarity that our seminar tries to study in depth. It is a vast world and a wide vision that would demand us to dwell upon the unity and variety of mysticism. Unity in diversity, the hallmark of Indian genius, is also the characteristic note of mysticism in general. The core of mysticism, I would think, is its unity in diversity. The interdisciplinary focus of our seminar is certainly very correct and relevant, and I do hope that our sessions, and sharing will stimulate more creative and critical thinking and make really innovative contributions towards the complimentarity of sciences. This is my fervent hope and prayerful wish on this happy and promising occasion.

2. Mysticism: One and Many

Mysticism, by its very nature, is an intimate and intense communion with the indescribable. It is a deep experience of the unseen and the unthought. Mysticism is essentially without bounds. It is in time and space; but enables man to go beyond time and space. Any study on religion and mysticism, in order to be valid and convincing, has to start from experience, from lived-religion and lived-mysticism. Our studies on mysticism have to be an unfolding of the latent layers of our daily lived-experience. "Nothing is more difficult to define than experience."[1] Experience gives us knowledge that we do not gain by reasoning and mediate evidence; it is a knowledge gained through our living union with things and persons. Human experience is the storehouse of all sciences. Of course science is a part of human life, and it naturally influences the course of experience, but experience is on the whole a pre-scientific process, very rich and comprehensive. However, every human experience has always authentic interpretations implanted in it. There is really no authentic human experience that is devoid of interpretations.[2] It is at the heart of human experience that sciences, both positive and human, ultimately find their complimentarity and mutually constitutive nature.

Mysticism is basically a profound experience of union with an ultimate reality encountered in manifold ways: through religious experiences, search for truth, and expansion of human consciousness with the help of world religions, all forms of sciences, various schools of philosophies and theologies. Mysticism finds its expression in art forms, and literature. It has its powerful expressions in its experiential encounter with Nature. As the deep encounters differ in their nature, so mysticism has its unity and variety. Within our experience, religious or not, there is an intimately connected common ground where boundaries

---

[1] Jean Mouroux, L'experience Chretienne, Paris: Aubier, 1952, 19.

[2] Jose M.de Mesa and Lode L.Wostyn, *Doing Christology*, Chicago: Claretian Publications, 1989, 25-30.

cross over, where unity and diversity meet and merge. It is the "stream of experience," in the words of William James, who stands for the variety of religious experiences. At the center of this stream there is an order and unity. Order and unity are not to be reposed on the stock of experience, but they are there; and the task of thought and reflection, the objective of our researches and studies is to clarify, to lay bare the connections and principles of order already given in immediate experience of mysticism. It is in this sense that we can perhaps say that phenomenology of mysticism is not constructive and deductive but more a descriptive analysis. Mysticism without bounds is cosmic in its nature and constitution, unity in diversity, One in Many and Many in One.

While reflecting on the nature and dimensions of mysticism, my thought goes to three eminent scholars who have classically discussed this subject, Rudolf Otto (*The Idea of the Holy*),[3] William James (*Varieties of Religious Experience*)[4] and R.C. Zaehner (*Concordant Discord*),[5] representing three different but complimentary schools of thought; namely the Unity school, the Variety school and Unity in diversity school respectively. To my mind, these three schools are mutually complimentary and inclusive. Mysticism, by its very essence, is mutually inclusive. Exclusiveness is alien to the very nature of mysticism. Hence I would think that mysticism has to lead us naturally to a cosmic consciousness and an all-inclusive vision that would strongly promote an interdisciplinary approach in our researches and studies. Serious and comprehensive studies on mysticism will contribute towards an integrated vision of man and his world and help us cultivate an attitude of convergence and collective consciousness.

In mysticism there is undoubtedly a religious layer in the inmost sanctuary of our life. It is a fusion of finite and infinite; it is a "sense and taste for the infinite."[6] (It is that basic experience that man, at his deepest level, is beyond space and time, beyond causation and earthly flux, as

---

[3] Rudolf Otto, *The Idea of the Holy*, Oxford: Oxford University Press, 1923.

[4] William James, *The Varieties of Religious Experience*, London: Allen and Unwin, 1968.

[5] R.C. Zaehner, *Concordant Discord: The Interdependence of Faiths*, Oxford: Clarendon Press, 1970.

[6] Schleiermacher, *On Religion*, Cambridge: Cambridge University Press, 1966, 46.

Aldous Huxley taught.[7] At the heart of mystical experience there is a mutually constitutive and complimentary merging of the material and the spiritual. For mystics, reality is both material and spiritual, having a within-dimension and a without-dimension, an inner dimension and an outer dimension, as Teilhard de Chardin, a paleontologist and a mystic, rightly tried to understand. His deep experience in the battle field during the World War II are evident examples of beautiful blending of science, philosophy and religion, all centered on the phenomenon of man. All mystical experiences are experiences of identity with that which is experienced. This identity-experience is the essence of all types of mysticism.

Mystical experiences are one and many, deriving from the vision and lived-world of every mystic. Mystics are people who have some immediate experience of the divine, of transcendence, of trans-temporal that gives them an inner, intense illumination. "The term 'mystical' has over a long period, been connected with the idea of union and participation."[8] Mystics are generally eminent people and they exercised a lasting influence on life in general and religious life in particular. Some of them have tried to describe their experience, to analyze its conditions and its effects upon the human personality. There are sharp divisions in this region of mystical experience which however, are difficult to explain as we find all sorts of gradations and mixtures.[9]

Mystical experience could perhaps be described as a divine or extraordinary 'shock' which takes place for different people in different ways, though often, it is an unsolicited experience. Some psychologists, like Abraham Maslow, call it a "peak experience,"[10] while others might say that it is a 'trip' or a 'kick'. The 'kick' means an ecstatic revelation, an experiential confrontation with God according to Timothy Leary.[11] Essentially, it is an extraordinary experience that makes man forget his sense of time and gives him a 'taste of eternity'. The curious and

---

[7] R.C. Zaehner, *Concordant Discord: The Interdependence of Faiths*, Oxford: Clarendon Press, 1970, 37.

[8] Ninian Smart, *The Yogi and the Devotee*, London: Allen and Unwin, 1968, 68.

[9] William James, *The Varieties of Religious Experience*, 301.

[10] A. Maslow, *Religions, Values and Peak Experience*, quoted in Peter Baelz, *The Forgotten Dream*, London: Oxford Mowvrays, 1975, 115.

[11] Timothy Leary, *The politics of Ecstasy*, London: Mac Gibbon, 242.

constructive component of mystical literature all over the world is that the description it gives, in spite of divergent interpretations, which depend upon the external milieu, has many things in common, though there are essential differences. All the mystics agree that what they experience cannot be expressed in words; if it is expressed in words then the sharpest paradoxes cannot be avoided. The 'opposites' are not so much abolished as transcended. Though there is a common and cosmic ground in mystical experience there are many types of mysticism, Hindu and Muslim, Sacred and Profane, Buddhist and Christian. Evidently the proponents of Nature Mysticism like: Walt Whitman[12] and R.M. Buck[13] did play an important role in the field of mysticism. The unity in multiplicity nature existing in all mystical experiences, whatever their differences are, is the best possible, common ground for the science of sciences, the foundation of all sciences, the science that transcends all sciences. This indeed, is a promising vision for opening new paths in researches and reflections.

3. Conclusion

This international seminar will hopefully contribute towards the new meanings and deep dimensions of the common ground in all mystical experiences of different traditions. The very nature of being in general is a unity in multiplicity. Interdependence and inner mutual complimentary structure are essential to the basic human consciousness and human experience. No human experience, mystical or otherwise, can be absolutely isolated. Togetherness is the focal point of human existence itself. Human beings are existentially inter-subjective, human experiences are deeply interrelated and coextensive. If Descartes, the Father of modern philosophy, could say that, "I think, therefore I am (*Cogito ergo sum*)", today we would perhaps say that "We are, therefore I am" (*Sumus ergo sum*). This inter subjective and co-existential structure in all human experiences and especially in mystical experiences will lead us to new paths in our intellectual pursuits and break new grounds in the field of sciences.[14] Mysticism can very well be converted into a

[12] Walt Whitman, *Song of Myself*, London: Nonesuch press, 1938.
[13] R. M. Buck, *Cosmic Consciousness* (23rd Edition), New York: E. P. Dutton, 1966.
[14] Pierre Teilhard de Chardin, *Writings in Time of War*, London: Collins, 1968.

very fertile field for new and creative studies; it will hopefully give us a new intellectual illumination and greater motivation for interdisciplinary researches. This is the innovative and inspiring motive of this seminar. Indeed, it is a very commendable collective attempt and I am sure, we will have wonderful findings at the conclusion of this great coming together of so many scholars. Mysticism opens our minds and hearts, deepens the depth of our very being and finally enlightens us from within.

Let our reflections and researches give us a new inner illumination so that we are able to understand the deeper ground of mysticism and the wider possibilities of inter-disciplinarity in our search for truth and new meaning of life, especially in the fast growing cross cultural context of today. Let us humbly become more aware that no science can afford to be isolated, exclusive, and exhaustive. Every science is in need of other sciences. Deeper awareness of the latent interconnectedness in all our experiences, especially in the mystical experiences, will throw more light on the still deeper roots of complimentarity and convergence. This will certainly help us to mould a brighter vision for the future.

Let us get more motivated from within, better committed to the search for truth and more enriched by our deep experiences of inner interconnectedness. Let us search together for new grounds for an interdisciplinary approach in our studies and researches. This is my fervent prayer and fond hope. Thank you.

3

Leonard Cohen's Poiesis

Toward the Unified Heart Where all Bounds Fade Away

Dr. Alexandra Pleshoyano
University of Sherbrooke, Canada

The road is too long
The sky is too vast
The wandering heart
Is homeless at last (Leonard Cohen)

Born on Friday September 21st 1934, Leonard Cohen grew up in Montreal, Canada, in a fervent Jewish family structured by religion.[1] According to the Jewish tradition, those born on a Friday are called for special piety. As a child Cohen attended the Hebrew School at the *Shaare Hashomayim* synagogue two afternoons a week and on Sunday mornings. He felt that it was *their* synagogue not only for religious reasons – being members of the Montreal Jewish community – but because both his paternal great grandfather and his grandfather had, in

[1] For more biographical information see: Tim Footman, *Leonard Cohen: Halleluja. A New Biography*, New Malden, Surrey: A Chrome Dreams Publication, 2009; David Boucher, *Dylan and Cohen: Poets of Rock and Roll*, New York/London: Continuum, 2004; Ira B. Nadel, *Various Positions: A Life of Leonard Cohen*, Austin: University of Texas Press, c1996, 2007; Jim Devlin, *In Every Style of Passion. The Work of Leonard Cohen*, New York: Omnibus, c1996; Loranne S. Dorman & Clive L. Rawlins, *Leonard Cohen: Prophet of the Heart*, London/New York/Sydney: Omnibus Press, 1990.

a large part, been its founders.[2] Lyon Cohen made sure that his children and grandchildren would receive a strong knowledge of Jewish history in order to respect their identity. This belief was passed on to Leonard. Moreover, the name Cohen is venerated in Jewish Culture, and Leonard was brought up being told that he was the descended from Aaron, the high priest, and was expected to become a leader of men.[3]

Leonard's maternal grandfather, Rabbi Solomon Klinitsky-Klein, was born in Lithuania and had been influenced by Hasidic Judaism, a mystical movement known to draw upon the resources of the *Kabbalah*. Cohen considered his grandfather to be a "*rebbe*" – a holy man – and enjoyed studying the *Book of Isaiah* with him particularly because this would give him time alone with him: a company he deeply appreciated. At the age of nine, Leonard went through a dramatic loss: his father Nathan died from a lung disease. The child was left with Esther, his older sister and Masha, their Russian mother. On the day after the funeral, Leonard wrote a message – his first poetic utterance – and after inserting it inside one of his father's bow ties, he buried the whole thing in the backyard of his Westmount home. He might have been thinking that his buried poem would have more easily reached his buried father. Recalling this, Cohen said: "I've been digging in the garden for years, looking for it. Maybe that's all I'm doing, looking for the note."[4]

A few years after his father's death, Cohen started to write notes to women to seduce them. And as he says: "They began to show them around and soon people started calling it poetry. When it didn't work with women, he says, I appealed to God."[5] Cohen was fascinated by

[2] The Cohens helped in the foundation of the *Shaar Shamayim* synagogue in Montreal, The Baron de Hirsch Foundation, the Zionist Organization, the *B'nai B'rith*, the founding of the Jewish General Hospital, the Hebrew Free Loan Society, and all the institutions connected with *Shaar Shamayim*. See *The Jewish Book News Interview* by Arthur Kurzweil and Pamela Roth, "Leonard Cohen. Stranger Music: Selected Poems and Songs". This interview was originally posted to alt.music.leonard-cohen by Martin Grossman (*tgg@bronze.coil.com*) on 31 October 1994. Formatted in HTML by carter page (*page@pobox.com*).

[3] David Boucher, *Dylan and Cohen: Poets of Rock and Roll*, 222.

[4] Leonard Cohen, *Stranger Music: Selected Poems and Songs*, Toronto, McClelland & Stewart Ltd., 1993, 207.

[5] Susan Lumsden, "Leonard Cohen Wants the Unconditional Leadership of the World" in *Weekend Magazine*, September 12, 1970, quoted by Nadel, *Various Positions: A Life*

women and thought they were all poets inhabited by "this highly charged landscape that poetry seemed to arise from."[6] This led him to believe that poetry could be the only way to address them. Some 'notes' appear to be poems, others made up novels, short stories,[7] and numerous ones ended up in songs. But all of them emerged from Cohen's inner well creating this one life-long work of art. The artist has kept on writing these "notes" for years and the longing for both women and God is ever present throughout his work. In 1949, he stumbled on a book of poems written by the Spanish poet Federico Garcia Lorca (1898-1936) which literally transformed young Cohen's life. He found something in there that just resonated in his own heart: "It was [a] universe that I already inhabited, so I claimed him as my brother."[8] Although the life of an artist is no picnic, Cohen could not get rid of the strong impression Lorca had made on him: "[…] once I knew that there was this landscape that he'd established, I wanted to stay there most of the time."[9] There was no turning back for him although he quickly turned away from the Academia as we shall see in the first part of this paper. From being a poet and a novelist, Cohen turned toward the popular music industry, where his own act of poiesis would emerge from. In the second part, we shall explain what we mean by the act of poiesis. This will bring us to the third part where Cohen's poiesis reflects this deep longing towards the unified heart where all bounds fade away. As the Jewish scholar, Elliot Wolfson, rightly points out, Cohen's poiesis is "infused with the mystical longing, of the disconsolate self to be absorbed in the limitless expanse of infinite light, to be reintegrated into the one that encompasses and is within all things."[10]

---

of Leonard Cohen, 3 and in Footman, *Leonard Cohen: Halleluja. A New Biography*, 19.

[6] *Songs from the Life of Leonard Cohen*, 1988.

[7] Many short stories can be found at the *Thomas Fisher Rare Book Library* in Toronto.

[8] Chris Doritos, *Interview with Leonard Cohen*, KCRW FM, Los Angeles, February 18, 1997. Transcription by Roxanna Bahro, www.leonardcohenfiles.com.

[9] Chris Doritos, *Interview with Leonard Cohen*, KCRW FM, Los Angeles, February 18, 1997. Transcription by Roxanna Bahro, www.leonardcohenfiles.com.

[10] Elliot R. Wolfson, "New Jerusalem Glowing. Songs and Poems of Leonard Cohen in a Kabbalistic Key", in *Kabbalah: Journal for the Study of Jewish Mystical Texts* 15 (2006), 110.

What do we mean by the act of poiesis? What is the process of it all about? Where does it spring from? How does it take shape? Could the act of poiesis help to reach a mystical state of consciousness where the divine light permeates all things and where all bounds disappear making the heart feel peaceful and unified at last? These are some of the questions addressed in this paper. I will conclude by bringing forth some concerns and ineluctable challenges that we are facing in our world of globalization.

1. From the Academia to the popular music industry

Now I've heard there was a secret chord
That David played, and it pleased the Lord
But you don't really care for music, do you? (Leonard Cohen)

In 1951, Cohen registered at McGill University. He showed poet and Professor Louis Dudek some of his poems, but Dudek was not at all impressed. A couple of weeks later, Cohen showed him a new poem entitled "The Sparrows" which immediately caught his professor's attention. As they left the classroom together and were walking down the corridor, Dudek stopped and commanded: "Kneel down." Feeling utter astonishment, young Cohen knelt down. Dudek then, using the rolled-up manuscript, dubbed him and commanded: "Arise. You are a poet. I have knighted you. Now you are one of us."[11] Cohen published his first book of poems in 1956; *Let us Compare Mythologies*, followed by a second in 1961, *Spice-Box of Earth* – a title referring to *Havdalah*, a Jewish religious ceremony. The latter was identified in 2006 as "one of Canada's 100 most important books."[12] To this day, Cohen has published twelve books of poetry – the latest being *Book of Longing* in 2006 – two novels, twelve music studio albums,[13] and six live music albums. Many other writings have not yet been published.[14]

Despite his books of poetry and novels, Cohen was mainly perceived as a singer/songwriter rather than as a poet and novelist. On the literary

[11] Dorman & Rawlins, *Leonard Cohen: Prophet of the Heart*, 52.
[12] Tim Footman, *Leonard Cohen: Halleluja*, 39.
[13] The latest being *Old Ideas*, Columbia Records, January 2012.
[14] Leonard Cohen's archives are being kept at the *Thomas Fisher Rare Book Library* in Toronto.

scene, he stopped being perceived as a poet as soon as he decided to pick-up the guitar and sing. As Stephen Scobie commented: "the more he is taken seriously as a 'rock star', the less seriously he is taken as a 'poet/novelist'."[15] In fact, many scholars had looked down on him when he undertook his career as a singer/songwriter. They perceived this singing career as a decline in his literary talent. Some critics were and still are virulent. Since then, Cohen openly rejects the label of poet.[16] Asked to explain his turning away from the academia, Cohen replied: "It's due to the process of cultural advertising which has the same effects as commercial advertising. Certain words become devalued and not only that but many people rush to embrace the description and I just don't like the company."[17] In his latest book of poetry, *Book of Longing* (2006), Cohen wrote: "Out of the thousands / who are known, / or who want to be known / as poets, / maybe one or two / are genuine / and the rest are fakes, / hanging around the sacred precincts / trying to look like the real thing. / Needless to say / I am one of the fakes, / and this is my story."[18] So Cohen bluntly refuses the title of a "poet" but nevertheless keeps writing his own act of poiesis. And don't ask him to comment on it for his answer will be: "I write the poetry, you do the commentary."[19]

It is no wonder if Cohen is not at ease with the academic environment where there is a persistent dichotomy between poetry and music. Universities and concert stages are obviously two separate genres of performances: the former for scholars and the latter for the common run of people[20]. This is typical of the Western way of separating sciences from humanities; the former considered as being 'objective' and the latter 'subjective'. As Guy Beck stresses: "Referred to as the 'old paradigm' by more progressive thinkers, this dichotomy of insider/

---

[15] Footman *Leonard Cohen: Halleluja*, 110. Footman interviewed Stephen Scobie in May, 2009.

[16] Despite such reluctance, Leonard Cohen won and accepted a top Spanish Literature award, the Prince of Asturias award in June 2011. The award's Jury said that Cohen had created 'imagery in which poetry and music are melded into an unchanging worth."

[17] Harry Rasky, *The Song of Leonard Cohen: Portrait of a Poet, a Friendship and a Film*, Oakville, Ontario: Mosaic, 2001, 66.

[18] Leonard Cohen, *Book of Longing*, **Toronto: McClelland & Stewart, 2006,** 73.

[19] Dorman & Rawlins, *Leonard Cohen: Prophet of the Heart*, xi.

[20] In August 2012, Leonard Cohen refused the title of Doctor *Honoris Causa* offered by Ghent University in Belgium.

outsider or musician/scholar, also known to anthropologists as emic/etic, has continued to inform attitudes for well over a century."[21]

Cohen acknowledges a difference between a poem and a song saying that the velocity is different. A poem takes place in silence even though the artist may hear rhythms in his mind. A poem can sit alone on a page unlike a song which has to move swiftly from the transmitter (the singer) to the receiver (the listener). Regarding his songs, Cohen says that: "There has to be space around the words, because you don't want to stop the mind, but belate the mind."[22] Words should be naturally woven across this great silence. What matters most is the appropriate relation between words and wordlessness. And wordlessness is much more important than all the words stringed together. The wordlessness is precisely where the listener or the receiver can experience a personal inspiration, a motion of the divine realm. Yet despite the differences between a poem and a song, both share a common feature: in each case comes the emergency to write. Scobie's opinion is that Cohen's songs "were more than poems put to music, that the lyrics and the music grew together to create a powerful personal utterance."[23] He perceives Cohen as being both a poet and a singer/songwriter: "The songs cannot stand apart from the poems."[24] For Cohen there is music everywhere and "that is the literature of our day, those lyrics, those songs, those rhythms are how people wash the dishes and court each other."[25] The American poet Kenneth Rexroth, views Cohen's writings – poems and songs – as an immense breakthrough: "This is certainly the future of poetry – he says, people poetry – direct, one to the other, I to Thou."[26] According to Rexroth, Cohen "accomplishes what the surrealists failed to do – his poetry is fundamentally subversive of the human sensibility.

---

[21] Guy L. Beck, "Introduction", in *Sacred Sound. Experiencing Music in World Religions*, Guy L. Beck (ed.), Waterloo, Ontario: Wilfrid Laurier University Press, c2006, 2009, 19.

[22] Martin Siberok, "Back in Demand" in *Montreal's Premier Cultural Tabloid*, vol. 1, Number 4/4, July 29 – August 11, 1988.

[23] Stephen Scobie, "Leonard Cohen" in *Studies in Canadian Literature*, Number 12, Vancouver: Douglas & McIntyre, 1978, 127.

[24] Tim Footman, *Leonard Cohen: Halleluja*, 110.

[25] Tim Footman, *Leonard Cohen: Halleluja*, 116.

[26] Dorman & Rawlins, *Leonard Cohen: Prophet of the Heart*, 213.

It is the voice of a new civilisation."[27] Linda Hutcheon for her part considers Cohen's work of art as "a product of a broader literary trend: the increased formal and thematic self-reflexivity of poetry today."[28] She believes that such a phenomenon has not been witnessed since the Renaissance, "such a marked and internalized concern for the craft of poetry and its relation to the art of living."[29] This combination between poetry and the art of living (*Levenkunst*), this powerful and inspired utterance, is precisely what we mean here with Cohen's act of poiesis.

2. The act of poiesis: an excruciating and fascinating process

Poiesis is straightaway conceived in the sense of differentiation and assimilation of perceptions, impressions and reminiscence that are improvisation of images not yet acknowledged as memories. The artist gets some impressions which in turn create inner and outer stimulations. Martin Heidegger uses the expression to refer to an act of breeding, to an act of production. He compares the act of poiesis to the blossoming of flowers and to the metamorphosis of the caterpillar to the butterfly. As Thomas Sheehan writes: "The unity of creation and preservation is art itself, which Heidegger calls *Dichtung* – not 'poetry' but poiesis, the creating-and-preserving installation of disclosure in a disclosive medium."[30] The act of poiesis represents the act of creating in the sense of transforming and extending the inner world of an individual, say the formal 'conversion' of his most profound inspiration. Whether it be through praises, poems, songs, drawing, painting or else, the act of poiesis gives form to an intuition or even to a mystical insight of the numinous.[31]

Intuition can grasp something of the eternal through the temporal, something of the infinite through the finite. If we cannot grasp the rational

[27] Dorman & Rawlins, *Leonard Cohen: Prophet of the Heart*, 213

[28] Linda Hutcheon, "Leonard Cohen," in *Canadian Writers and their Works*, Toronto: ECW Press, 1992, 32.

[29] Linda Hutcheon, "Leonard Cohen," 32.

[30] Thomas Sheehan, "Heidegger, Martin (1889-1976)," *The Short Routledge Encyclopedia of Philosophy*, Edward Craig (ed.), London & New York: Routledge, 2005, 366.

[31] See Rudolf Otto, *The Idea of the Holy*, Oxford: Oxford University Press, c1923, 1958.

meaning of it, it is simply because this is not given to the exercise of the intellect, of the conceptual, but rather to the world of the intuition where the feeling is regarded as a means of knowledge. In other words, intuition brings a subtle light for those who have eyes to perceive it and who possess the ability to transform such a formless intuition into an artistic and tangible form although such form will always remain far short of the reality of the original experience (*Erlebnis*). The act of poiesis renders a finite and limited form which always remains at the threshold of this original experience. Throughout all time, in music as well as in other artistic fields, these forms send back to another reality, one that surpasses infinitely our rational world. The experience of the numinous is never immediate, but rather mediated by those who experience it, those who interpret it and give shape to it. The act of poiesis can therefore become a means to give a form to an intuition which at first is formless. Cohen has no choice, he says, but to follow *the course from chaos to art,*[32] from chaos to cosmos and order. He has to find a sufficient voice to give life to these songs burgeoning within him. Through the process of poiesis hides a mysterious will which inspires the artist and the mystic. But the origin of such an inspiration remains unknown; it appears to some as supernatural and divine, to others it may be associated to the natural realm.

Be it natural or supernatural, the act of poiesis is usually a painful process often compared to labor pains. The struggle of writing, for example, can be very hard and demanding on the writer. As Cohen explains: "If it is your destiny to be this labourer called a writer, then you know that you've got to work every day, but you also know that you're not going to get it every day."[33] In fact, says Cohen, it is a predicament for which the artist must be prepared: "You really don't command the enterprise."[34] Cohen doesn't consider poetry as an occupation or an intention but as a verdict.[35] He writes from his own predicament facing his alternating alienation and fulfillment, desolation and elation, longing and desertion, repetitive depressions and moments of peace: all of his

[32] See Leonard Cohen, *Book of Longing*, **Toronto: McClelland & Stewart, 2006, 1.**

[33] *Leonard Cohen: I'm Your Man*, Lian Lunson (dir.), Lionsgate Films, 2006.

[34] *Leonard Cohen: I'm Your Man,* 2006

[35] See Brian D. Johnson, "Life of a Lady's Man" in Maclean's, December 7, 1992, 64.

frequent ups and downs. Cohen's act of poiesis is quite a struggle but he "has always been someone to extract wisdom from twists of fortune, be they shattered romances or corruption in society; some of his best songs are built upon sharp insights into human nature gained when on the ropes."[36] Cohen writings are scraped out from the bottom of his heart. Being an artist is certainly not an easy way of living. As he says: "If you are interested in being an artist and you intend to do serious work then you are going to have to spend a lot of time in the ditch."[37] And if someone is not prepared to do just that then he should forget it. If one is really called to be an artist, said the German poet Rainer Maria Rilke, then he will have to shoulder that destiny and bear it – both the burden and the greatness – without ever asking what recompense might come out of it.[38] An artist, in Cohen's opinion, is someone who speaks to people deeply and sincerely and to do so the artist has to realize that there is a large share of suffering in everyone's life and that these people need works of art that will name their predicaments and perhaps transcend them. But there are no two ways about it: either you deal with the suffering or you're just never going to be an artist, says Cohen.[39]

Referring to the frequent feeling of abandonment and desolation that every artist undergoes, Cohen adds: "What was the second last thing Christ said? 'Why hast thou forsaken me?'"[40] Cohen experiences the act of writing as an ordeal: "I have always had the sense of being

[36] Simon Houpt, "Coffee and Candour with Cohen" in *Globe and Mail*, Toronto: February 27, 2009. A good example of this is his sudden return to the public scene in the spring of 2008 motivated by the misappropriation of five million dollars by his former manager, Kelley Lynch. Cohen is grateful that he could still make a living at 73 years old, but even more grateful are those millions of people who could and still can assist to his concerts since then. Cohen doesn't recommend to anyone the loss of everything as a form of "spiritual discipline," but he adds: "if it happens to you there are some features that are quite surprising and quite nourishing." Cf. Brian D. Johnson, "Halleluja" in *Uncut*, December 2008, 57.

[37] Aaron Shuster, "Leonard Cohen. Calm after the Storm" in *Campus Digest*, September 1984.

[38] Cf. Rainer Maria Rilke, *Letters to a Young Poet*, trans. by M.D. Herter Norton, New York: W.W. Norton & Company Inc., 1940, 18-19.

[39] Cf. Aaron Shuster, "Leonard Cohen: Calm after the Storm" in *Campus Digest*, September 1984.

[40] Quoted by Hustak, "Bird on a Wire; Leonard Cohen, at 60, has donned the cloak of New age prophet," D11/Break.

bone-dry."[41] He can't compare himself to a Dostoevsky who could write a novel within a few months: "I never experienced the torrent of creative force that other people have spoken about – the ground doesn't move."[42] A year later, Cohen described the act of writing as something even worse: "It's something like scavenging, something like farming in sand, something like scraping the bottom of the barrel."[43] He certainly doesn't see any dignity in such a process but an "extreme poverty."[44] He says that: "the process is really more like a bear stumbling into a beehive or a honey-cache: I'm stumbling right into it and getting stuck, and it's delicious and it's horrible and I'm in it. And it's not very graceful and it's very awkward and it's very painful."[45]

In a 1996 video made on Mount Baldy by Arnelle Brusq, Cohen compared this process of writing to the practice of zazen: "Things arise that are very, very disturbing. And there's no way around it, there's no way over it, there's no way under it, there's no way to the side of it, there's no way of forgetting it."[46] Cohen experiences both zen and the process of writing as an intolerable disorder in his life. He says: "You have to sit in the very bonfire of that distress and you sit till you're burned away and it's ashes and it's gone."[47] This "death" of the ego appears as the only narrow way to the act of poiesis. The poet Rilke could spend months feeling oppressed by a sensation of influenza, incapable of doing or writing anything.[48] But then again as the German poet wrote: "A work of art is good if it has sprung from necessity. In this nature of its origin lies its judgment; there is no other."[49] Thus the writing process springs out of emergency. Cohen feels that this emergency is a process that seems to last forever bringing him most of the time into a chaotic and unbearable state of mind. In an interview with Alan Hustak, he says

---

[41] Johnson, "Life of a Lady's Man", 65-66.

[42] Johnson, "Life of a Lady's Man", 65-66.

[43] Ian Pearson, "Growing Old Disgracefully" in *Saturday Night*, March 1993.

[44] Ian Pearson, "Growing Old Disgracefully," 1993.

[45] Pico Lyer, "Leonard Cohen Unplugged," in *Buzz, Los Angeles*, April 1998, available on the leonardcohenfiles.com

[46] Leonard Cohen: Spring 96, Armelle Brusq (dir.), Lieurac Productions, 1997.

[47] Leonard Cohen: Spring 96, 1997.

[48] Rainer Maria Rilke, *Letters to a Young Poet*, trans. by M.D. Herter Norton, New York, W.W. Norton & Company Inc., 1940, 21.

[49] Rilke, *Letters to a Young Poet*, 18.

that: "The emergency never ends. At times a peaceful self is born, but it never lasts, it never lasts." The preliminaries of writing torment the artist excessively, triggering the feeling of his brain being confused and struggling "at the bottom of a well, trying to find something that will give a song permanence in this world."[50] This condition is not an option: it's a question of both a personal and professional survival. And Cohen went on asking: "How do you escape the cycle? How can I find a sufficient voice to give life to these songs? It is a situation where luxury has no place, where only urgency is concerned."[51] In his poem entitled *Thing*, Cohen writes: "I am this thing that needs to sing / I love to sing / to my beloved's other thing / and to my own dear sweet G-d/[52] I love to sing to Him and her / […] /O G-d I want to sing / I Am / THIS THING THAT NEEDS TO SING."[53] Cohen needs and loves to sing to G-d (God) and to her, the woman, *all* women.

Cohen is aware that his poems and songs are being given to him but doesn't know where it comes from; if he knew he would go there more often. "There is only one thing that I've learned over the years, he says, only one artistic rule I've ever been able to develop, and that's stick with it. Because eventually it will yield."[54] Cohen gets his messages across reaching the hearts and minds of many. He has always felt that the nature of a song was a movement from lip to lip, heart to heart. It is not designed to remain fixed on a page like a proper poem but it moves by nature.[55] The Baal Shem Tov "considered singing a service of God, for music touches the soul and produces an outpouring of the soul."[56] Cohen's intention is to make his poetic songs sound the way read poems do. He wants his poetic songs to flow both melodiously and accurately. He also stresses the sacramental relationship between musicians and

---

[50] Christian Fevret, « Comme un guerrier » in *Les Inrockuptibles*, August 21, 1991.
[51] Christian Fevret, « Comme un guerrier », 1991.
[52] In order to respect his Jewish Religion where it is forbidden to pronounce the Name of God, Cohen uses the abbreviation: "G-d".
[53] Cohen, *Book of Longing*, 112.
[54] Siberok, "Back in Demand."
[55] Cf. Dorman & Rawlins, *Leonard Cohen: Prophet of the Heart*, 185.
[56] Yitzhak Buxbaum, *The Light and Fire of the Baal Shem Tov,* New York: Continuum, 2008, 150-151.

audience.[57] He offers his act of poiesis to the common run of people. He feels like a channel at times through which inspiration flows. He says: "When you become the work itself [...] you don't stand aside you're just the instrument of the energy and there's no second thoughts."[58] Cohen feels called on to offer his songs to this mysterious divine woman (perhaps the *Shechinah* which represents the female emanation of God for the Jews) as shown in the following poem entitled *Basket*:

> You should go / from place to place / recovering the poems / that have been written for you, / to which you can affix your signature. / Don't discuss these matters / with anyone. / Retrieve. Retrieve. / When the basket is full / someone will appear / to whom you can present it. / She will spread her wide skirt / and sit down /on a black stone /and your basket will bounce / like a speck in sunlight / on the immense landscape / of her lap.[59]

Cohen is a lover, but now he is called to become the loved one: "You have loved enough, / Now let me be the Lover."[60] The *Lover* (with a capital 'L') in Cohen's poiesis refers to G-d [God], the divine love. And as he said in a recent interview: "The older I get, the surer I am that I'm not running the show."[61]

In 1984, Cohen published a very personal book entitled: *Book of Mercy*[62] which, he says, is literally an act of prayer. It is the end result of all he had been doing so far and it sprang from an inner need. The "book is the result of my devotion to my God and to a religious tradition [Judaism]."[63] Cohen says that the book came about at a time when he felt blocked-up and silenced, feeling the urge to encounter the source of mercy and forgiveness in his life. And he adds: "That's what these

---

[57] Cf. Dorman & Rawlins, *Leonard Cohen: Prophet of the Heart*, 369.
[58] Walker, Billy, Complexities and Mr. Cohen, in *Sounds*, March 4, 1972, http://www.leonardcohenfiles.com/sounds2.html
[59] Cohen, *Book of Longing*, 51.
[60] Cohen, *Book of Longing*, 55.
[61] Rohter, "On the Road, for Reasons, Practical and Spiritual".
[62] Leonard Cohen, *Book of Mercy*, Toronto: McClelland & Stewart Ltd., 1984.
[63] Dorman & Rawlins, *Leonard Cohen: Prophet of the Heart*, 326.

psalms are about – trying to locate that source of mercy that enables you to re-enter the world."[64] Mercy in Judaism refers to an act of kindness. And the ultimate act of kindness for the Jews is to sanctify the Name of God which is precisely what Cohen intended with his book by addressing the Name (capital "N") (*ha-Shem*). Cohen's book had first been entitled *The Name*, then *The Shield* and finally *Book of Mercy*. Judaism insists indeed that the secret of existence is a "Who?" not a "What?" question. Addressing God's name is therefore a matter of intimacy, an act of love. Cohen blesses[65] the Name which lies beyond all capacities of comprehension. Calling out God's name unlocks the understanding of the heart.[66] Only an open heart filled with God's mercy can be lifted to the infinite mystery of the name of God (Ex. 3:14). As Arthur Green writes: "The only place you have to travel to find God's word is to your own heart. The journey to the heart is precisely the mystical[67] quest."[68] And the biblical psalmist writes: "I will raise him up because he knows my name" (Ps. 91:14). This rising from God is usually viewed as a fall in the eyes of men as psalm # 8 in *Book of Mercy* proves:

> IN THE EYES OF MEN HE falls, and in his own eyes too. He falls from his high place, he trips on his achievement. He falls to you, he falls to know you. It is sad, they say. See his disgrace, say the ones at his heel. But he falls radiantly toward the light to which he falls. They cannot see who lifts him as he falls, or how his falling changes, and he himself bewildered till his heart cries out to bless the one who holds him in his failing. And in his fall he hears his heart cry out,

---

[64] Dorman & Rawlins, *Leonard Cohen: Prophet of the Heart*, 325.

[65] "Bless" and "blessing" are among the most frequent terms used in Cohen's *Book of Mercy* (60 times).

[66] The word "heart" is among the most cited words in Cohen's *Book of Mercy* (65 times).

[67] "Mystical" here is to be heard in the sense of God's mystery. The mystical quest refers to all those who are looking to deepen their search of God. As Green writes: "Mystics are often thought to be people who have great supernatural religious experiences, who see the room fill with light or the heavens alive with angels. [...] I have no such experiences to share with you, dear reader". See Arthur Green, *EHYEH, A Kabbalah for Tomorrow*, Woodstock, Vermount: Jewish Lights Publishing, 2002, xii.

[68] Green, *EHYEH, A Kabbalah for Tomorrow*, 21.

> his heart explains why he is falling, why he had to fall, and he gives over to the fall. Blessed are you, clasp of the falling. He falls into the sky, he fall into the light, none can hurt him as he falls. Blessed are you, shield of the failing. Wrapped in his fall, concealed within his fall, he finds the place, he is gathered in. While his hair streams back and his clothes tear in the wind, he is held up, comforted, he enters into the place of his fall. Blessed are you, embrace of the falling, foundation of the light, master of the human accident.[69]

Cohen's psalm echos Eckhart's idea of detachment which "is a radical reorientation achieved through realisation of the nothingness of the created self, a realisation that also implies abandoning the God who punishes and rewards."[70] This loving God is holding Cohen while he falls. This falling is not of this world as nobody can possibly "fall into the sky". As Bernard McGinn underlines this negation of detachment is concentrating "on our letting go of *our*[71] desire, though by releasing not by striving."[72] Such form of negativity is recurrent in Cohen's *Book of Mercy*.

Shortly after the publication of *Book of Mercy*, Cohen was interviewed by Robert Sward who was struck by the relative absence of will in those psalms. Doesn't one need a will to pray or to write a psalm, he asked Cohen? The latter answered that we are called to be a reflection of the greater will that is behind everything. When "our own tiny will comes into contact with that greater will, it undergoes a lot of battering. We are then thrown back into a kind of silence"[73] until we can make contact with another authentic thrust of our being. And if we can affirm such an experience, says Cohen, then we call it a prayer.

---

[69] Cohen, *Book of Mercy*, Psalm # 8.

[70] Bernard McGinn, "Three Forms of Negativity in Christian Mysticism" in *Knowing the Unknowable. Science and Religions on God and the Universe,* ed. John Bowker, London: I.B. Tauris, 2009, 111.

[71] Underlined in the text itself.

[72] Bernard McGinn, "Three Forms of Negativity in Christian Mysticism," 102.

[73] Robert Sward, "Interview with Leonard Cohen," Montreal, Quebec, 1984. Available at leonardcohenfiles.com.

This is what happened to him in *Book of Mercy*, he says.[74] The book is a good example of this sort of emergency: "It is speaking directly from the heart and one is lucky when that happens."[75] And he went on to say: "It is a prayer. And you can only begin a prayer when there are no other possibilities."[76] Conscious that our modern society is anything but religious, Cohen says: "when you find yourself forced to your knees and asking for help, this only happens when it's true. And that book [*Book of Mercy*] came out of that predicament."[77] Many psalms in *Book of Mercy* reflect this state of total surrender to God. Surrender here refers to a form of kenosis, an emptying of one's self which reveals itself in splendid fashion as the deepest communion between the self and the Absolute.

Cohen refers to his book as being a Book of Psalms:[78] "not that we need another, he says. But I just wanted to sing and dance before the Lord[79]." This reminds one of the Hasidic Founder, the Baal Shem Tov[80] (the Besht), who told his disciples that: "The holy Zohar says that there are heavenly palaces whose gates are only opened by song." And he went on saying: "But you have to sing before God, and let the *Shechina*[81] [the female emanation of God] sing through you. When you dance, dance before God."[82] Thus Cohen's music opens halls in the heavens for his audience many review his concerts as being a spiritual

[74] Robert Sward, "Interview with Leonard Cohen," Montreal, Quebec, 1984.
[75] Aaron Shuster, "Leonard Cohen. Calm after the Storm" in *Campus Digest*, September 1984.
[76] Aaron Shuster, "Leonard Cohen. Calm after the Storm" in *Campus Digest*, September 1984.
[77] Aaron Shuster, "Leonard Cohen. Calm after the Storm" in *Campus Digest*, September 1984.
[78] According to the Jewish scholar, Robert Alter, *mizmor* is the Hebrew word for "psalm" and it refers to something being sung and to the verb *zamer*, which means singing or hymning.
[79] Paul King, "Leonard Cohen mixes movie-making and Zen" in *The Gazette*, Montreal: Saturday, July 16, 1983.
[80] Rabbi Israël ben Eliezer was born in 5458 (1698 CE) – 5520 (1760 CE) in a small village, Okop, in Ukraine on the Polish Russian border (Podalia). He became known as the Baal Shem Tov (Master of the Good Name) and is the Founder of Hassidism which is possibly the most important religious movement in the Jewish history.
[81] For the Jewish mystics the *Shechinah* is the female emanation of God.
[82] Yitzhak Buxbaum, *The Light and Fire of the Baal Shem Tov*, 151.

experience or a form of ecstasy. "Just as in the dance, [writes Gerardus van der Leeuw] ecstasy is one of the means of expressing the other, reaching a new reality. [...] Music, freeing itself from the world, rises up to heaven in silent or occasionally loud ecstasy."[83]

Throughout his work, Cohen bears witness to a constant longing bringing together love, sensuality, spirituality and creativity. As he says and sings: "It is in love that we are made. In love we disappear."[84] His good friend, Jennifer Warnes, says that: "If he [Cohen] has one great love, it is his search for God."[85] In 1964, when an undergraduate student asked Cohen what made a poem, he answered: "God" and he added: "It's the same kind of operation as the creation of the world."[86] The act of poiesis can indeed be viewed as a gift of God. As Edward Foley wrote: "[...] music has symbolized the mysterious and wholly other since the dawn of creation." And Foley went on writing that: "In the Judeo-Christian tradition music is an effective means for communicating with a God who is both present and hidden."[87] Prayers portray images of a mystery that transcends all possible representations. Trying to explain Cohen's wide success, Eli Mandel writes: "It may be the appeal of a certain kind of religiosity in his work that accounts for this phenomenon."[88]

Regarding the meaning of his prayer-songs, Cohen usually remains elusive and discreet. As he says: "[i]t's difficult to do the commentary on the prayer, [...] I feel it doesn't serve the enterprise to really examine it from outside the moment."[89] In other words, prayers for Cohen are infinitely intimate and their deepest meaning always remains in the sphere of the ineffable. The mystery of a prayer can never be divulged. In the like of the mystics, Cohen experiences the limits of linguistic but paradoxically language remains the only accessible way to that which

[83] Gerardus van der Leeuw, *The Holy in Art*, New York: Rinehart and Winston, 1963, 233.

[84] Cohen, *Book of Longing*, **64.**

[85] Larry Rohter, "On the Road, for Reasons Prartical and Spiritual" in *New York Times* (February 24, 2009).

[86] Quoted by Nadel, *Various Positions: A Life of Leonard Cohen,* 129.

[87] Edward Foley, "Music, Liturgical" in *The New Dictionary of Sacramental Worship*, Peter E. Fink, ed. Collegeville MN: Liturgical Press, 1990, 868-869.

[88] Eli Mandel, *Five Modern Canadian Poets*, Toronto/Montreal: Rinehart & Winston of Canada, Limited, 1970, 73.

[89] Rohter, "On the Road, for Reasons, Practical and Spiritual".

cannot be spoken. Perceiving the mystic as a singer, Henri Corbin[90] writes that although "the mystic must sing in order to say, since mystical meaning is essentially musical, this meaning still remains ineffable."[91] And he adds that: "As soon as we make so bold as to communicate it, to reveal that fugitive instant where it seems that 'the soul becomes visible to the body,' then the secret escapes us."[92] According to van der Leeuw: "Music leads into the depths of life, there where the boundaries flee away."[93] Thus Cohen's act of poiesis allows him from time to time to reach a state where his heart is peaceful and unified at last, a state where all bounds fade away.

3. The unified heart where all bounds fade away

So what about this Inner Light
That´s boundless and unique?
I´m slouching through another night
A thousand kisses deep[94] (Leonard Cohen)

The primordial Word of God, the Torah, bears both the divine love and the divine light revealing whatever one is able to carry. The presence of God throughout the world is true since the beginning, but it exists in the form of hidden light, a divine light that permeates the whole universe but is accessible only through a mystical state of consciousness. The divine light shines everywhere and all of us are but refractions of its glow. Cohen's song, entitled *Love itself* reflects this experience of a unified heart where all bounds between one and the Other fade away.

---

[90] Henri Corbin (1903-1978) was a philosopher, a theologian and professor of Islamic Studies at the Sorbonne in Paris, France.

[91] Henry Corbin, *The Voyage and the Messenger: Iran and Philosophy,* trans. Joseph Rowe, Berkeley: North Atlantic Books, 1998, 235-36, quoted by Elliot R. Wolfson, *Venturing Beyond. Law & Morality in Kabbalistic Mysticism*, New York: Oxford University Press, 2006, 243.

[92] Henry Corbin, *The Voyage and the Messenger: Iran and Philosophy,* 235-36.

[93] Van der Leeuw, *The Holy in Art*, New York: Rinehart and Winston, 257.

[94] Cf. *Blackening Pages* at http://www.leonardcohenfiles.com. Page consulted on 2 December 2011.

The light came through the window,
Straight from the sun above,
And so inside my little room
There plunged the rays of Love.
In streams of light I clearly saw
The dust you seldom see,
Out of which the Nameless makes
A Name for one like me. [...]

Then I came back from where I'd been.
My room, it looked the same –
But there was nothing left between
The Nameless and the Name.[95]

With this song, Cohen witnesses of the overcoming of all the usual barriers between the Nameless and the Name, between the No-thing and the All. In such a state of consciousness, Cohen feels as if he has become One with the Name, One with G-d. For just a brief moment, God's divine light is no longer hiding behind successive layers of veils. In a poem entitled *You Are Right, Sahara*, Cohen writes:

> […] There are no mists, or veils, or distances. But the mist is surrounded by a mist; and the veil is hidden behind a veil; and the distance continually draws away from the distance. That is why there are no mists, or veils, or distances. That is why it is called The Great Distance of Mist and Veils.[96]

Cohen's poems and songs often echo these polarities. Life is entwined in opposites and contradictions but Cohen tries to connect all

---

[95] Mont Baldy 1997-2001. Cf. *Blackening Pages* at http://www.leonardcohenfiles.com. Page consulted on 2 December 2011. This song is also available in *Song Index*, *Love Itself*, on the album *Ten New Songs*, 2001, at http://www.leonardcohenfiles.com. Page consulted on 3 December 2011. The song here is dedicated to *L. W. which refers to Leon Wiesentier*. Read the first chapter from Leon Wieseltier's book *Kaddish* and reviews by Harold Bloom in The New York Times and Robert Fulford in Toronto's *Globe and Mail.*

[96] Cohen, *Book of Longing*, 44.

the contradictions and paradoxes, reuniting it into his act of poiesis. Although this world is full of irreconcilable conflicts, Cohen actually believes that there aren't any conflicts and that everything could be reconciled if we manage to reach an attitude of complete surrender, of "total affirmation."[97] He goes on saying that there are actually moments when we can transcend the dualistic system and reconcile and embrace the whole mess and that's what he means by 'Hallelujah! Blessed is the Name.[98]

The influence of the Scriptures is omnipresent throughout Cohen's writings. In a recent documentary entitled "I'm Your Man", Cohen says that his interest in poetry was first inspired by listening to the chanting of Jewish prayers and to the recounting of bible stories in the synagogue.[99] Indeed Cohen openly acknowledges his indebtedness to Jewish tradition. In his article entitled "New Jerusalem Glowing", Elliot Wolfson discusses the songs and poems of Cohen in the key of the symbolism of kabbalah.[100] When Wolfson asked Cohen if he had studied kabbalah or Hasidism, and if he acknowledged a direct influence of either of these spiritual disciplines on his work, Cohen replied that he had a very superficial knowledge of the matter but even by only dipping into the many books, he had been deeply touched by what he had read, and by his conversations with living Hasidic masters:

> The model of the Tree of Life [he says] and the activities and interactions of the sephirot has been especially influential. The idea of the in-breath to clear a space for the whole manifestation and the out-breath as the place of the manifestation, has of course been illumined by my studies with Roshi, my old Buddhist friend and his instructions in zen meditation.[101]

---

[97] "How The Heart Approaches What It Yearns", Interview with John McKenna, RTE, May 9, 1988).

[98] Cf. Cohen, *Book of Mercy*.

[99] Cf. *Leonard Cohen: I'm Your Man*, Dir: Lian Lunson, Lionsgate Films, 2006

[100] Elliot R. Wolfson, *Venturing Beyond Law & Morality in Kabbalistic Mysticism*, New York: Oxford University Press, 2006, 103.

[101] Elliot R. Wolfson, *Venturing Beyond*, 103-104, footnote #2.

Referring to the *Sefiroth* – the Jewish mystical Tree of Life – Cohen says that only one side of it, mainly *Gevurah* representing justice and judgement, is being strongly supported whereas the other side, *Hesed*, symbol of love and mercy, is being neglected. The kabbalists in Jewish mysticism represent the divine pleroma as the Tree of life with ten creative and powerful attributes which reflect the intra-divine life. "But [as Gershom Scholem underlines] these images in which God is manifested are nothing other than the primordial images of all being."[102] The realm of the *Sefiroth*, says Scholem, can only be spoken of "in the language of symbols, since it is not accessible to the direct perception of the human mind."[103] As Wolfson writes:

> [...] in the mind of kabbalists all things in the universe are viewed symbolically as images of the sefirotic potencies, but the latter are themselves symbolic screens upon and through which the boundless and indeterminate light is projected and refracted, a light that cannot be delimited as light without ceasing to be the light that is to be delimited, a light that comprehends darkness not as its antinomy, nor as a reflection of the same, but as the identically different that is differently identical.[104]

In the like of both the Sefirot and the doctrine of *coincidentia oppositorum* attributed to Nicholas Cusanus in fifteenth century, Cohen affirms the identity of opposites by means of their difference. By his notion of *coincidentia oppositorum*, Cusanus argued that two poles with opposite qualities subsist at the same moment and are both first and last at the same time. Cohen perceives everything as being connected: all the paradoxes of his life are reunited at one point or the other. This reminds of a quote written in 1909 by the American philosopher William James a year before his death:

---

[102] Gershom Scholem, *On the Kabbalah and Its Symbolism*, with a new Foreword by Bernard McGinn, New York: Schocken Books, c1965, 1996, 100.

[103] Gershom Scholem, *On the Kabbalah and Its Symbolism*, 35.

[104] Elliot R. Wolfson, *Language, Eros, Being. Kabbalistic Hermeneutics and Poetic Imagination*, New York: Fordham University Press, 2005, 7

> [...] our lives are like islands in the sea, or like trees in the forest. [...] But the trees also commingle their roots in the darkness underground, and the islands also hang together through the ocean's bottom. Just so there is a continuum of cosmic consciousness, against which our individuality builds but accidental fences, and into which our several minds plunge as into a mother-sea or reservoir.[105]

But who can live forever underground or at the bottom of the ocean? These special moments cannot last for long but whoever experiences them keeps a profound and everlasting inner impression. Many mystics will compare such an experience to an inner burning wound that remains printed within them forever even though they may not experience it with the same intensity. As Meister Eckhart says, "it is possible to attain an inner state that remains immovable the way the hinge of a door remains in one place as the door opens and shuts."[106] Indeed there seem to be a particular state of consciousness where lie potential forms of consciousness that are totally different from the rational consciousness and this is what we mean by the mystical states of consciousness. As William James once wrote: "No account of the universe in its totality can be final which leaves these other forms of consciousness quite disregarded."[107] These mystical states of consciousness are strikingly discontinuous from the ordinary consciousness and keep us from all premature conclusions regarding truth and reality. Cohen seems to ascribe these to some divine significance and an appeal for reconciliation. As James writes: "It is as if the opposites of the world, whose contradictoriness and conflict make all our difficulties and troubles, were melted into unity."[108]

As we have argued in this paper, Cohen's music has this power of joining people together from different religious and non religious background into the "oneness" of a spiritual realm, strengthening thereby

[105] William James, Archives, VII.8 WJ: "The confidences of a 'psychical researcher'." Autograph manuscript, signed, [1909], bMS AM1092.9 (4545): "In this essay, published in the *American Magazine* in October, 1909."
[106] Bernard McGinn, "Three Forms of Negativity in Christian Mysticism," 111.
[107] William James, *The Varieties of Religious Experience*, [electronic version available online, 308].
[108] William James, *The Varieties of Religious Experience*, 308.

a kinship spirit as if by some uncanny thread. Cohen always stresses the fact that we are all part of a brotherhood under the Almighty and that any form of exclusivity appears as wholly unacceptable. "A confident people is not exclusive [he says]. A great religion affirms other religions. A great culture affirms other cultures. A great nation affirms other nations. A great individual affirms other individuals, validates the beingness of others."[109] Cohen adds that there is something nonnegotiable about the absolute that fits in with his most rigorous and deepest longing about the matters of which he was taught. And the purest expression of that reality, he says, is expressed in the *Shema*: "Hear, O Israel: the Lord our God, the Lord is one" (Deut. 6:4). Cohen believes in an absolute unity that is manifesting itself on this plane and on all planes. Zen appears mainly to him as a method, a landscape on which Jewish practitioners – and others – can manifest their deepest longing concerning the absolute. All that matter really to Cohen is that Zen Buddhism can provide a space for him to do the kind of dance with the Lord that he can't find in other places.[110] Despite his more than forty year involvement with Buddhism, Cohen still cherish his Jewish identity: "Anyone who says I'm not a Jew is not a Jew, I'm very sorry but this decision is final."[111] Nevertheless, Cohen has always been quite critical toward the Jewish institution saying that the messianic unfolding has not been asserted enough and that the mercy of the Lord is neither sufficiently affirmed. He rejects all the exclusive visions which affirm only one side of humanity despising the other. As he writes in his poem entitled *Tired* published in 2006:

> We're tired of being white and we're tired of being black, and we're not going to be white and we're not going to be black any longer. We're going to be voices now, disembodied voices in the blue sky, pleasant harmonies in the cavities of your distress. And we're going to stay this way until you straighten up, until your suffering makes you calm, and you can believe the word of G-d who has told you so many times, and in so

[109] Wolfson, *Venturing Beyond*, 105-106.

[110] Kurzweil and Roth, "Leonard Cohen. Stranger Music: Selected Poems and Songs".

[111] Cohen, *Book of Longing*, 158.

> many ways, to love one another, or at least not to torture and murder in the name of some stupid vomit-making human idea that makes G-d turn away from you, and darken the cosmos with inconceivable sorrow. We're tired of being white and we're tired of being black, and we're not going to be white and we're not going to be black any longer.[112]

If one asks Cohen today if he is religious, his answer will probably be negative because he doesn't want to confine his faith to dogmas and matters of a specific doctrine where others may be excluded. But should we limit the word "religious" to the institutional? The word religion refers to two different aspects: the systematization of thought and concepts on the one side – which does not interest Cohen – and lived religious experience with its symbols and images on the other side. Cohen is mainly interested by the latter and this is why he has no difficulty to conciliate what may appear as disparate components, like the Buddhist method of meditating, the feminine divine figures in Christianity and the Tree of life in the kabbalah. Cohen seems to perceive someone like the Virgin Mary as a manifestation among others of the *Shekhinah* – being the last rung of the *Sefiroth* and the feminine presence of God on earth. As Wolfson rightly points out, the similarities that we can acknowledge between Cohen and Jewish esotericism can only be fully appreciated against the other philosophical and religious traditions like Zen Buddhism and Christianity which had important effects on his [Cohen] act of poiesis.[113] Indeed, writes Wolfson: "the poet [Cohen] both expands and constricts the boundaries of his Judaism vis-à-vis other traditions in an effort to legitimate the validity of the other on the basis of affirming the distinctiveness of his own cultural formation."[114] This is certainly one of the biggest challenges for the interfaith dialogue in our world of globalization. Let us conclude.

---

[112] Cohen, *Book of Longing*, 124.
[113] Wolfson, Venturing *Beyond,* 105.
[114] Wolfson, Venturing *Beyond,* 105.

4. Conclusion

In this paper, we saw that both the artist and the mystic are aware of the impossibility to express adequately both the wholly Other and the wholly Same. As Martin Buber writes: "Of course God is the 'wholly Other', but He is also the wholly Same, the wholly Present. Of course He is the *Mysterium Tremendum* that appears and overthrows; but He is also the mystery of the self-evident, nearer to me than my *I*."[115]

We find in poetry and music an inclination to silence which connects it with mysticism. Here lies the constant tension between apophatism (wordlessness) and cataphatism (wordiness): "For all true music is dramatic, [writes van der Leeuw] and moves, like all art, in eternal movement and countermovement between form and formlessness."[116] The point where music and religion intersect with each other "lies between art and service. Voices represent something; they do not sound for themselves, but for something else."[117] The artist and the mystic are actually acting as instruments of God, attending to the wholly O/other. As Otto writes: "Musical feeling is rather (like numinous feeling) something 'wholly other', which, while it affords analogies and here and there will run parallel to the ordinary emotions of life, cannot be made to coincide with them by a detailed point-to-point correspondence."[118] Both the artist and the mystic know that only silence could adequately express the wholly O/other, but they still need to utter their inspiration. The silence between the words and the chords are by no means something negative, but the negative expression of something most positive, [writes van der Leeuw]. It is, in genuine mystic fashion, a rich poverty, a full emptiness [...] a "sacramental silence."[119] As William Barnard writes: "[P]erhaps, this recognition of our limits will impress upon us not only the need for a tolerance of differences, but also the value of methodological modesty, as well as a certain bottom-line respect for the

[115] Martin Buber, *I and Thou*, trans. Ronald Gregor Smith, New York: Charles Scribner's Sons, second edition, 1958, 79.
[116] Van der Leeuw, *The Holy in Art*, 256.
[117] Van der Leeuw, *The Holy in Art*, 261.
[118] Rudolf Otto, *The Idea of the Holy*, 49.
[119] Van der Leeuw, *The Holy in Art*, 237.

sacredness of the individual."[120] Art – through all its forms – remains the most appropriate tool to utter the inexpressible because it allows silence and empty spaces within its structure and it welcomes paradoxes and irreconcilable elements. By keeping silent, one is not being inactive, but is being receptive in its highest activity.

Years ago, Cohen had founded a movement called *The Order of the Unified Heart* without any intention of founding a sect or becoming a guru of some kind. Cohen is too aware that this longing towards a unified heart where all bounds fade away could never take shape through any form of dogmas but is strictly something that each one of us has to work on by his self and try to share it with others. Cohen's poiesis may help to reach this unified heart. As Robin Sylvan writes, the "musical experience is a unique mode of being-in-the-world in which the dualities of subject-object, body-mind, and spiritual-material are transcended in a unified field."[121] Music has the power to transcend radical divergences between people and to exhibit a startling degree of cross-cultural agreement. From George Steiner's point of view, music plays a central role in understanding humankind: "Our capacities to compose and to respond to musical form and sense directly implicate the mystery of the human condition. To ask 'what is music?' may well be one way of asking 'what is man'?."[122] Indeed, since the origins of humankind, the act of poiesis – through music amongst other forms – has been a medium to relate the everyday experience, keeping track of history in general. Cohen's openness and respect toward the mystery and sacredness of each individual make his work highly valuable for the interfaith dialogue in a world of globalization. According to Buber: "He who truly goes out to meet the world goes out also to God."[123] At 78 years old, Leonard Cohen still finds the energy to travel around the world giving concerts and sharing his most inner self. Perhaps is it his way today to meet with both the world and God?

---

[120] G. William Barnard, *Exploring Unseen Worlds. William James and the Philosophy of Mysticism*, New York: State University of New York, 1997, 68.

[121] Robin Sylvan, *Traces of the Spirit. The Religious Dimensions of Popular Music*, New York/London: New York University Press, 2002, 215.

[122] Georges Steiner, *Real Presences*, Chicago : University of Chicago Press, 1991, 6.

[123] Martin Buber, *I and Thou*, 95.

Our world of globalization is quite a challenge for those who wish to truly meet the other without any prejudice of any kind. But how can we perceive the other as being identically different and differently identical? Could we affirm our own identity without excluding anyone? This is quite a challenge, not just for religious reasons, but for all the spheres of our being. And yet, isn't it the only way to go if we want to live and survive in our world of globalization? Perhaps we need to learn anew what it means to listen (*hineinhorchen*): listen to our most inner being in order to listen to the most inner being of the others!

4

Negative Memory, Art and the World Peace

Dr. Ignatius Bambang Sugiharto
Parahyangan Catholic University, Indonesia

The world peace has always been connected to politics or law, but rarely to art. While the importance of art for human soul is generally acknowledged, its connection with wider human socio-cultural life is often unrecognized. Negative experience in general, or negative memory in particular, can be taken as the bridge connecting art to world peace. This paper will explore the negative memory and experience: how they are related to the possibility of world peace, and how the arts, especially in its new development, can play significant role.

1. Negative Memory and its Vicious Circle

Memory is the guardian of the ultimate dialectic of historicity, that is, the dialectic between the past, the present and the future. Memory renders the past constitutive of the present. By means of memory, history becomes history of the present. In terms of existential meaning and value, the past is not something merely elapsed or superseded, but rather, the 'having been' of an unfinished project, a part of an incomplete ideal, a mission to accomplish.

In the writing of history, keeping memory alive is tantamount to an 'act of sepulcher', 'an act of repeated entombment', a ritual, with its prolonged mourning;[1] a celebration of continuity vis-à-vis, or despite, the discontinuity. Negative memory, in particular, renders the discourse of history critical, hence 'critical history', where negative memory is never to remain a mere fact, but rather, to be taken as a protest demanding critical recognition. This means, negative memory is not to be viewed as a simple *mnêmê* – a spontaneous irruption of images of an event into awareness- , but rather, an *anamnesis* –an act of recollection. In this way negative memory expands collective memory, even corrects and criticizes the actual memory of a community. The work of negative memory is successful not only if it gives rise to a resurrection of the past, but above all, if it emancipates us from the negative past.

The dilemma, however, is that, as a negative experience, the memory is always at the risk of self-censorship or being deliberately forgotten. Indeed, as *mnêmê,* memory is always in the midst of the undecidable polarity between forgetting through effacement and forgetting through reservation, between *ars oblivionis* and *ars memoriae,* between destruction and construction, amnesia *and anamnesis.*[2] Ricoeur calls this 'the irreducible equivocalness' of forgetting, of which 'there is no possible balance sheet'.[3] As in the case of mass destruction or genocide (Holocaust, Hiroshima, Khmer Rouge, etc) the suffering is such that the negative memory, the experience of negation, is oftentimes really unforgettable. Hence there cannot be a happy forgetting in the same way as a happy memory; no possible balance sheet. On the other hand, if *anamnesis,* memorization or not-forgetting, means perpetuating vengeance, history will remain locked up within the deadly oscillation between eternal hatred and forgetful memory. It is here that forgiveness comes to be imperative. Forgiveness is the rational way out of the deadly oscillation between the memory of suffering or hatred and absolute forgetting. To break the vicious circle of anamnesis and *amnesia* there

---

[1] This is a poetic terminology used by Paul Ricoeur in emphasizing the moral responsibility for the past. The work of mourning separates the past from the present and makes way for a better future. See Paul Ricoeur, *Memory, History, Forgetting, trans*. Kathleen Blamey et al, Chicago: The University of Chicago Press, 2004, 499.

[2] Cf. Paul Ricoeur, *Memory, History, Forgetting*, 503-5.

[3] For Ricoeur, it is 'equivocal' in the sense that there is no superior point of view from which one could perceive the common source of destruction and of construction. Paul Ricoeur, *Memory, History, Forgetting*, 503.

must be *amnesty*. Like *amnesty*, forgiveness is the silencing of the non-forgetting memory, the ceasing of vengeance, the forgetting of the unforgettable, the negation of negation.

2. The Role of Art

Forgiveness, in turn, requires a transformation of memory, from memory as affection into memory as reflective recognition, from *pathos* to *logos*. Forgiveness requires the belief in the power of reflection and speculation over the irreparable. And the most effective means to render possible such transformation is the arts: monument, film, theatre, painting, novel, poem, etc. Through its capability of touching the heart, the soul and imagination, art has the potential to expose the irreducible equivocalness of negative memory, and at the same time to transcend the pain as well as to transform its destructive forces; it is capable of interweaving, in a recuperative and re-creating manner, the burden of the past, the attention to the present, and the expectation of the future. Art brings the past into gestures of inauguration, as in rituals of initiation, for the sake of a new beginning, a new way of looking at things. It is no coincidence that in this case the term 'memory' or 'forgetting' is often related to the word 'art' as in the terms of *ars memoriae* and *ars oblivionis*.

In this context, however, art is neither simply concerned with skill (*ars, tékhnê*), nor merely with beauty, but rather, with 'creation', creating a new perception (*poeín*, *aísthesthai*); or even further, it is concerned more with 'truth', be it in the Kantian sense of the 'sublime', in the Psychoanalytic sense of the 'subliminal', or even better, in the Heideggerian sense of *alêtheia*, that is, truth as the disclosure or the openness of new possibilities of meaning and of being in the world: truth as the lighting and concealing of beings.[4] Art is the "setting-itself-into-work of truth", the creative preserving of truth. Creative in that it brings the unsayable or the unthinkable into being, and simultaneously re-creates what is ordinary, defamiliarizes what is familiar, and in so

[4] See Heidegger, "The Origin of the Work of Art" in David F. Krell, ed. *Martin Heidegger, Basic Writings*, London: Routledge & Kegan Paul, 1978,184.

doing transforms our accustomed ties to the world, hence the opening up of new possibilities of looking at things.[5]

To see whether or not art today is still capable of accomplishing the mission of revealing such truth, however, we have to consider first some significant changes in the world of contemporary art. The striking phenomena, among other things, are the contemporary tendency of art to eliminate its stasis and object-centred character in favor of interactive process, its tendency to dissolve itself in the banality of life, and its excessive obsession with violence, pain, terror, and *thanatos* in general. While this has returned art to its primal habitat, it also requires new modes of appreciation.

3. Art Today

Today, when we come to the contemporary practices and experiences of the arts, our initial fascination often turns into bafflement, for the arts confront us with a disconcerting array of materials and perceptual activities. Traditional aesthetic theory seems at loss in front of the works of art with new materials, such as plastics, acrylics, gas, chemical ingredients, telepathic power, holographic images; electronically produced sounds; novels and plays without plots, and so on and so forth. And even basic distinctions within the arts fail to hold, for we are no longer able to draw the line between design, decoration, illustration, and fine art, or let us say, between musical sound and noise. Art seems no longer content with its special venues and discrete forms, but intrudes on building walls, subway stations and city streets. The perceptual modalities required for the appreciation of art have also changed and have broken out of conventional patterns. At times we have to enter into the space of the art work, as in environmental sculpture; contribute to its process, as in interactive theatre, installation or performance-art, etc. This involvement with the art objects and in the aesthetic processes, in turn, suggests a participatory attention or 'aesthetic engagement' in the place of the traditional account of 'disinterestedness'.[6] The enlargement

---

[5] This is the 'poetic' character of all the arts, which, like 'naming' by language, it bestows, grounds and sets up a new beginning of being in the world. Heidegger, "The Origin of the Work of Art," 186.

[6] 'Aesthetic Engagement' is the term coined by Arnold Berleant in his effort to redefine 'Aesthetics' in terms of contemporary phenomena of the arts. See, Arnold Berleant,

of aesthetic sensibility has produced the deliberate elimination of perceptual distance between the artist, the work and the viewer. Henceforth art becomes more a process of creative interplay rather than a stasis.

But the more significant change is the integration of art and life in general, especially in the usage of the materials of everyday life. The music of John cage uses sounds of all sorts and considered any kind of noise as musical material. There are Happenings or Performance-art which deliberately draw their themes and materials from the ongoing course of ordinary life. 'One could view everyday life itself as theatre' says Cage. Pop art plays with the intimate relation between art and life. Robert Rauschenberg denies, for example, any division between what he calls 'Sacred Art' and 'Profane Life' and insists on working 'in the gap between the two'. Indeed, as he once remarked, 'There is no reason not to consider the world one gigantic painting'. Theatre, too, has joined the other arts here. Everything is a fitting subject, and in the most candid, graphic terms, from race relations to homosexuality, deformity, and the sex act. The distancing logic of a plot has receded and in its place the focus is on the ordinary details of life that we never trouble to notice, such as the series of movements by which a man sits in a chair, or a woman handles a cup or moves her lips, etc. All this illustrates what has become a motif in the twentieth-century art: a deliberate dethroning of art and its reintegration into the course of normal human activity.

Thus, the world of contemporary art has been characterized by the extension of the art object, the intensification of appreciative experience, the enlargement of art to include the total environment.[7] Corollary to this is the significant shift of focus from objects to process and awareness. What counts in art today is not the object in itself. The object may be absorbed into the totality of the aesthetic field or even 'disappear', in the case of 'non-object' art, like conceptual art or social project. The art object is a means, an instrument, for the heightening of perceptual awareness and the intensification of experience. The object can even

---

Rethinking Aesthetics, Hampshire: Ashgate Publishing Limited, 2004, 9.

[7] Arnold Berleant sees this as stages of evolution of awareness, which I take simply as different characters with no distinct period or stage. Cf. Arnold Berleant, *Rethinking Aesthetics*, 111.

be anything. This may sound like a radical upheaval from the point of view of conventional aesthetics, but this new development is perhaps simply a return to its origin. For art in its earliest meanings, as we can still find particularly in pre-modern societies, was neither the cultivated fineness of high civilization nor a matter of disinterested contemplation on a particular works of a genius, but simply the shaping, the joining together, and the celebration, of things, for the sake of infusing human feeling, imagination and meaning into them. It is a sort of multiplication and proliferation of human soul in various activities; sundry modes of incarnating the spirit in the world of things. It is a matter of sensitivity to the qualitative shape of human experience in their surrounding world, but also of various efforts to re-create the world in accordance with human aspirations. This explains why in the pre-modern life, as it is also now, the arts include any practices of creative human activity, such as festivals, crafts, ceremonies and rituals, even the culinary arts, the art of gardening, the art of flower arranging, etc. It is not without reason if today we still retain this general meaning of 'art' in the terms such as the art of conversation, the art of management, the art of politics, etc.

Indeed art has no longer any frame or distinct boundaries, for now it encompasses the whole range of human activities. While it might look like a degradation of aesthetics, it may precisely indicate the opposite: the radicalization of aesthetics, the aestheticization of life and environment. In this kind of art, it seems that the traditional key-concepts such as beauty, the sublime, contemplation, technical ingenuity, or formal configuration are no more central. Perhaps what is essential in art today is precisely its 'poetic' character, poetic in the sense of 'making' and 'creating' life itself. For sure here 'making' in the sense of 'craftsmanship' is retained, even extended and broadened, but what counts even more is creative making in its deeper sense: that the formless experience is given a form, the unsayable is articulated, the imaginable is made conscious, the conscious is made perceivable and tangible. And equally essential is the converse: the visible is set in the invisible, what is tangible and seen is connected to the untouchable and the ungraspable. This surely echoes the basic thoughts of Heidegger, but also in line with John Dewey's emphasis on the centrality of experience in the appreciation of art.[8]

4. Art and Negative Experience

Notwithstanding its positive side, taken at its face value indeed the art of the twentieth century may well show a serious degradation in that it is so much characterized by terror, cruelty, brutality, perversion, folly, void, necrophilia or thanatophilia, and includes all kinds of abjections. Just take for example, the actionism of Rudolf Schwarzkögler who cut his penis to death; self-destruction of Paul Celan, Chris Burden or Mark Rothko; theatre of cruelty of Artaud; the suspension of the pain of living of Stelarc's body-art; or , more recently, the exhibit of 200 human corpses by Günther von Hagens , to name only a few of them. In this sense, contemporary art is undoubtedly the art of negative experience par excellence. In its 'decomposition' or 'dematerialization', art derives its power not from a sense of unity, but from the intimation of the fragmentary, the broken. Rather than suggesting wholeness or redemption, it represents the breach itself, the ongoing need for reconciliation and forgiveness, while at the same time claiming its impossibility and becoming emblematic of its sufferings. Art-work becomes a token of the absence of meaning, of a void; the void made palpable.

All this negativity, however, cannot be attributed exclusively to the arts, for the art-world is itself the expression of the broader cultural body, albeit it also feeds back into and affects the culture, in subtle ways. Therefore, when we talk of contemporary art, what is important, yet often neglected, is contemporary cultural symptoms.

In fact the cultural atmosphere at the end of the second millennium was marked by depression, desacralization of life and human body, and disenchantment of the modern secular world, due to the absurdity of two World Wars. Modern transactions of meaning and value had also resulted in the invalidation of traditional frames of symbol, hence the loss of symbols, which, in turn, has generated the difficulty in articulating profound existential experiences. The extremity of art correlates also with the praxis of extreme sciences, that –like extreme sports- were

[8] Cf. John Dewey, *Art as Experience,* New York: Perigee Books, 1934, Ch. II & XIV.

striving some pointless experimentations transgressing the limit, by creating a life genetically programmed and producing abnormal chimera of all kinds. The shock of images, the meaninglessness of words, the overexposure of obscenity and folly in the art world were basically also analogous to the desensitization by the media that was exploiting the 'spectacle of abjection' or 'reality show', with its fake documents and conjuring tricks, simply in order to gain high ratings.[9]

Thus, our problem today is not concerned simply with the memory of certain negative experiences, but rather, with the whole general mode of existence of the past to the present, which seems to be severely saturated with negativity. Today the situation is even exacerbated by the production of fear, contradictory certainty and intolerance toward differences. Hence there exist terrorism, solidification of identity, paranoia, xenophobia, and genocide. Nevertheless, art does not simply express the negativity, that is, the void, the chaos, or the spiritual blindness of the socio-cultural plight. It may serve also as a diagnostic tool for identifying the disease; a process of intensifying and heightening our perceptual awareness of the crises; a necessary visualization of the critical interface between body, mind and soul; a process of integrating the dark side -the shadow- into human psyche; and an essential mapping of the extremes of human desire and consciousness. Art renders palpable the ugliness, the meanness, the unbearableness of life, and this, in turn, will open the possibility to see what ultimately is more desirable, the deeper mystery of soul, the new and different possibilities of existence, what we usually call 'peace'.

5. Art, Forgiveness and Peace

Whatever it may mean, 'peace' can be taken as a sort of umbrella term for anything emancipatory, for any expectation of a better future, for more meaningful and more desirable quality of coexistence with the 'other'. When negativity is not mere memory of the past, but rather, the general human condition of today, then the focus should be the expectation of the future, while the agent is anonymous, a matter of complex web of interrelationship in which the whole human race are involved and

[9] For more insight into the correlation between the arts and the modern cultural plight see Paul Virillio, *Art and Fear,* Trans. Julie Rose, London: Continuum, 2003, 50-55.

take part. In this context 'forgiveness' would mean 'negation of the negation' in the sense of, first, seeing the negativity as the clue toward what is more desirable, which otherwise remains unknown; second, negating the impossibility for us to be the perpetrator, and recognizing the possibility that the ultimate root of the negativity may be our very selves: each of us is the agent, not the victim. And here art plays double role. First, by means of its intimacy with negativity, the art discloses this truth of human illusions, sufferings and dreams, somehow that they can be personally recognized, in somatic, cognitive, imaginative or even spiritual way. Second, the integration of art with the daily life returns the poetics of the ephemeral, the sensibility to see further beyond banality, the celebration of ever new beginning, the courage to re-create one's own life in accordance with higher ideal. And thereby art becomes again the procreation of human soul in their sundry activities. Yet, when all is said, one still wonders whether without beauty and transcendence, art will really be able to help humans transcend their own trap or reach the desired 'peace'.

5

Confronting God 'As Such'

Between Poetry and Phenomenology in the 'Mysticism' of Derrida

Dr. Colby Dickinson
Loyola University, USA

1. Introduction

For Immanuel Kant, the regulative principle of the *as if* (*als ob*) was essentially all we have to work with in the world of representations.[1] We must accept, he contended, that things can only be comprehended *as if* they are what we perceive them to be, in their representational form. The presentation of a thing *as such*, that is, without its representative mediation, was something inaccessible, and therefore beyond what we are capable of understanding. Ever since, for most philosophers, who indeed often act as guardians of what is considered both possible and impossible within the realm of experience, this limitation has been enough to constrict our understanding of what is 'other' to us, that is, what is typically our own, varied reconstruction of whatever is presented

[1] Immanuel Kant, Lectures *on Logic,* trans. J. Michael Young, Cambridge: Cambridge University Press, 2004, 590-91. See also, his *Critique of Pure Reason*' eds. and trans. Paul Guyer and Allen W. Wood, Cambridge: Cambridge University Press, 1997, 525. His work subsequently influenced Hans Vaihinger, whose response to Kant's ethics in 1911 was entitled *The Philosophy of As If: A System of the Theoretical, Practical, and Religious Fictions of Mankind*, trans. C.K. Ogden, London: Routledge, 1965.

(or *re*-presented) before us. This is to say, practically speaking, that no *thing* can present itself beyond our representations.

Despite this seemingly insurmountable obstacle imposed upon us by structure of thought itself, recent trends in philosophical reflection have in fact sought to go beyond this Kantian restriction (or 'regulation') in order to experience something of a presence beyond representation. Nowhere has this dramatic search been more present than in the realm of poetry, where language continuously circles around the 'thing itself', asking it to come forth and present itself *as such*.

In what follows, I hope to illuminate the tensions between the regulative *as if* and the almost hyperbolic *as such* which attempts to extend itself beyond what we can and do represent both *in* and *through* language. To do so, I will be drawing first, though briefly, upon the poetic legacies of the *as such* in the poetry of Wallace Stevens and Adrienne Rich before turning to the post-Kantian philosophy of Jacques Derrida developed in a productive tension with the poetry of Paul Celan. In this fashion, I am hoping to illuminate the provocative contrast between poetic efforts aimed at revealing the 'thing itself' *as such* and Derrida's insistence upon the necessity of remaining indebted to the *as if*. In doing so, I am aiming as well to highlight the realm of the mystical as it is apparently produced in the tensions between these two worlds of re/presentation.

2. The poetic presentation *as such*

It could be said that there has always been within poetry an effort to capture and portray the 'thing itself' *as such*, an object as it is in itself, beyond whatever significations we humans can place upon it through our words. This is a doubly difficult task to perform as poetry is continuously immersed in a project to expose the existence of language and our relation to it, the shape and contours of this co-existence as well as its capabilities and shortcomings. In the work of the Italian philosopher, Giorgio Agamben, for example, there has recently arisen an intense desire to present (not *re*-present) 'The Thing Itself', something he finds at work in the philosophy of Plato as much as in the varied poetries of Dante, Rainer Maria Rilke or Giorgio Caproni, to name but a few.[2] If anything, what Agamben draws our attention to, time and again in his writings, is the failure of language to adequately *present* anything, and how therefore we become witness to a poetic drive to go beyond its inscriptions.[3] This is as much a theological issue, we might add (and as Agamben himself does add), as anything else.

This impulse to discern the 'thing itself', the *as such*-ness of a thing beyond its linguistically-codified and intelligible form, is what pushes many modern poets to tangle with the failure of language itself, what the American poet Adrienne Rich, for one, has often pursued under many names: the 'dream of a common language', the 'school among the ruins', and perhaps most poignantly, as an act of 'diving into the wreck'. It is in this last poetic image in particular that we are witness to what is perhaps the poetic task *par excellence*. As she describes the act of diving into a vast ocean in search of the sunken wreck of a ship that comes to mirror our daily lives as we have constructed them, she discovers:

> the thing I came for:
> the wreck and not the story of the wreck
> the thing itself and not the myth
> the drowned face always staring
> toward the sun
> the evidence of damage
> worn by salt and away into this threadbare beauty
> the ribs of the disaster
> curving their assertion
> among the tentative haunters [...].[4]

---

[2] Giorgio Agamben, 'The Thing Itself' in *Potentialities: Collected Essays in Philosophy*, trans. Daniel Heller-Roazen, Stanford: Stanford University Press, 2000, 27-38. See also, on 'the thing itself' and its relation to metaphor and representation, in Charles P. Bigger, Between Chora *and the* Good: *Metaphor's Metaphysical Neighborhood*, New York: Fordham University Press, 2005.

[3] Cf. 'How this push beyond language' is determined as a site of our potential 'infancy' according to Agamben. See Giorgio Agamben, *Infancy and History: On the Destruction of Experience*, trans. Liz Heron, London: Verso, 1993.

[4] Adrienne Rich, "Diving into the Wreck," Diving *into the Wreck: Poems 1971-1972*, New York: W.W. Norton, 1973, 23-4.

Echoing themes she will elsewhere describe as a having to deal with a patriarchical language that is yet her own, the 'oppressor's language', as Paul Celan will also call it, Rich seeks to move beyond language, its story and its dominion, in order to examine what lies before her, without words being used either to conceal or to distort it.[5] As she will parallel this movement in another poem entitled 'An Atlas of the Difficult World', nearly 20 years later,

> [...] I don't want to know
> wreckage, dreck and waste, but these are the materials
> and so are the slow lift of the moon's belly
> over wreckage, dreck, and waste, wild tree frogs calling in
> another season, light and music still pouring over
> our fissured, cracked terrain.[6]

In this return to the wreck, the ruin, the dreck, and the waste that is our language and that is all we have to communicate with, Rich is yet seeking something beyond language, a presentation of the beings that we are *as such*.

It comes as little surprise, then, that Rich spends some time, toward the end of the collection of poems entitled *Diving into the Wreck*, mediating on the figure of a 'savage child' (or 'feral child'), one discovered in the woods after having spent years without language, a possible infanticide gone terribly awry. There she looks to this solitary, wordless figure still bearing the scars of a knife once placed upon his throat as a sort of obverse mirror to our desires for immersion in both language and culture. She imagines, for example, how his 'rescuers' in fact, hoping to do the right thing,

---

[5] Adrienne Rich, "The Burning of Paper Instead of Children," *The Will to Change: Poems 1968-1970*, New York: W.W. Norton, 1971. On Rich's relationship to language in general, see Jane Hedley, "Surviving to Speak New Language: Mary Daly and Adrienne Rich," *Hypatia* 7:2 (1992), 40-62.

[6] Adrienne Rich, "An Atlas of the Difficult World," *An Atlas of the Difficult World: Poems 1988-1991*, New York: W.W. Norton, 1991, 4.

[…] tried to care for you
tried to teach you to care for objects of their caring […]

to teach you names
for things you did not need […]

to teach you language:
the thread their lives were strung on […].[7]

What these meditations produce for Rich, however, is not necessarily sympathetic to the 'rescuers' of this wayward 'savage' child. Rather, she is prompted through the contemplation of this figure to push beyond language, *to a place prior to language*, a place which recalls Agamben's attempts to locate an originary state of 'infancy' beyond our linguistic being. As she continues in the same context,

Go back so far there is another language
go back far enough the language is no longer personal

these scars bear witness
but whether to repair or to destruction
I no longer know […].[8]

This impulse to go beyond, because *before* language is not something unique to Rich's work. There are numerous poetic examples which could be invoked as prior attempts to push language to its limits and to work, through language, *beyond* language. Indeed, the desire itself seems to stem from those same regions which Agamben's work points to and which is immanently discernable in the poetry of one of Rich's greatest influences, her 'liberator' as she puts it: another American poet, Wallace Stevens.

In an essay devoted to tracing the influence of Stevens' poetry upon her own work, Rich tells us that 'It was he [Stevens] who said to

---

[7] Adrienne Rich, "Meditations for a Savage Child," *Diving into the Wreck*, 55-6.
[8] Adrienne Rich, "Meditations for a Savage Child," 58. On Agamben's concept of 'infancy', see his *Infancy and History*.

me, *Ourselves in poetry must take their place*, who told me that poetry must change, our ideas of order, of the romantic, of language itself must change…'.[9] Poetry has the power to break through the divisions of our world (such as that of gender, or race, which she specifically addresses in this context), and to offer something beyond these linguistically-encoded significations. And this is what Stevens, on numerous occasions, attempted to point toward himself, writing poems with such metaphysical tones as 'Reality Is an Activity of the Most August Imagination', 'The Poem That Took the Place of a Mountain', 'The Course of a Particular', 'The Role of the Idea in Poetry', 'Two Illustrations That the World Is What You Make of It', 'Of Mere Being', and, perhaps making the point best, his poem 'Not Ideas About the Thing But the Thing Itself'.[10] It is in this last poem, for example, that he inches ever closer, though the presentation of a thing *as such*, to what he calls 'a new knowledge of reality', that is, one stationed beyond the confines of the regulative logic of representations.[11]

It is a new knowledge of reality, then, that opens up new sources of access to the selves that we are, sources that almost paradoxically stem from the things themselves (beyond being reduced to either subjects or objects). We are caught up in the *as such*-ness of things, inescapably bound to them, though not identified through, with or in them. As the philosopher Simon Critchley has put it in a study of Stevens' poetry:

> The poetic act, the act of the mind, illumines the surface of things with imagination's beam. This act is part of the thing and not about it. Through it, we detect what we might call *the movement of the self* in those things: plate, bread, wine, water, rock, tree, and moon. In poetry, the making of things is

[9] Adrienne Rich, "Rotted Names," What *Is Found There: Notebooks on Poetry and Politics*, New York: W.W. Norton, 2003, 202. See also, Barbara L. Estrin, "Space-Off and Voice-Over: Adrienne Rich and Wallace Stevens," *Women's Studies* 25 (1995), 23-46.

[10] All poems can be found in Wallace Stevens, *Collected Poetry and Prose*, New York: Library of America, 1997.

[11] Wallace Stevens, "Not Ideas About the Thing But the Thing Itself," *Collected Poetry and Prose*, 452.

makings of the self. Poets are the chanting-hearted artificers of the world in which they sing and, singing, make.[12]

Perhaps what poetry really does, and what both Rich and Stevens attempt to point us toward through their poetry, is to present something beyond those signified representations with which we are so familiar, which help us to limit and identify our cultural frameworks, but which also violently reduce the fullness of any singularity appearing before us. The poetic self is one rather open to the things before it, letting them shape it as much as it shapes them. This is, as Philippe Lacoue-Labarthe describes in the context of Paul Celan's poetry, to point to the relevance of the *gesture*, or that which is somehow able to signify something yet at a remove from the realm of signification.[13] It is an attempt to *present* the 'thing itself' without reducing it to a common linguistic-symbolic marker. Poetry can thus attempt to *say existence itself*, and at the same time to express something of the 'catastrophe of language', something more than familiar to Rich's poetic endeavors to explore the wreck alongside the contamination of language.

3. Derrida and Celan on poetic meaning

Though these remarks on a possible poetic gesture beyond representation or signification may seem to be at a good remove from general thoughts upon the mystical, I am here wagering that, in fact, this poetic endeavor lies at the center of what we have often considered the mystical to be. It is an encounter with a presentation beyond our rationalized representations, something at the heart of most philosophical reflection over the last century or so as well.[14] I would also assert that this connection lies at

[12] Simon Critchley, *Things Merely Are: Philosophy in the Poetry of Wallace Stevens*, London: Routledge, 2005, 10.

[13] Philippe Lacoue-Labarthe, *Poetry as Experience*, trans. Andrea Tarnowski, Stanford: Stanford University Press, 1999, 50-1. See also, what is perhaps the only critical study available at present on the work of Lacoue-Labarthe: John Martis, *Philippe Lacoue-Labarthe: Representation and the Loss of the Subject*, New York: Fordham University Press, 2005, as well as Alison Ross, *The Aesthetic Paths of Philosophy: Presentation in Kant, Heidegger, Lacoue-Labarthe, and Nancy*, Stanford: Stanford University Press, 2007.

[14] Cf. Ross, *The Aesthetic Paths of Philosophy*, as well as the work of Jean-Luc Marion, to name but one example of such a conjunction. See Jean-Luc Marion, *Being Given:*

the heart of the work of the French philosopher Jacques Derrida, for whom the act of representation put forth through language, through the *text* which is all we have ('there is nothing outside the text'), is indispensible to our identities as subjects. For Derrida, in fact, who followed Kant closely in this, there is only the *as if* of representations, the strong metaphors of language upon which our constructions of self are dependent. We are inseparably connected to this reality, no matter how greatly we might wish to be separated from it. Indeed, in some sense, any attempt to be sovereign (politically) seems to stem, for him, from the attempt to remove oneself from the linguistic binds that hold us all in check.[15]

Derrida also famously said that his work was not a negative theology.[16] Negative theology so often leads to a presence; it invokes a (transcendent) presence through its prayers and in this sense is to be considered as a form of mystical thinking, of mystical theology as well as a sovereign theology or a theology of sovereignty. What Derrida is seeking to get at, for his part, however, is the structure behind (and beyond) theology, the existence of language as it has shaped and conditioned our every theology: 'Language has begun without us, in us, before us. This is what theology calls God, and it is necessary, it will have been necessary

---

Toward a Phenomenology of Givenness, trans. Jeffrey Kosky, Stanford: Stanford University Press, 2002. His conceptualization of the 'saturated phenomenon' is merged in his work with a certain understanding of mysticism; see his introduction to Michael Kessler and Christian Sheppard, eds. *Mystics: Presence and Aporia*, Chicago: University of Chicago Press, 2003.

[15] Cf. Jacques Derrida, *The Beast and the Sovereign*, eds. Michel Lisse, Marie-Louise Mallet, and Ginette Michaud, trans. Geoffrey Bennington, Chicago: University of Chicago Press, 2009.

[16] Jacques Derrida, 'How to Avoid Speaking: Denials'. *Psyche: Inventions of the Other*, Vol. II, eds. Peggy Kamuf and Elizabeth Rottenberg, Stanford: Stanford University Press, 2008, 147. Kevin Hart, for one, has utilized the notion of 'negative theology' in relation to Derrida's work in his *The Trespass of the Sign: Deconstruction, Theology and Philosophy*, Cambridge: Cambridge University Press, 1989. For an essay attempting to critique Hart's tendency to read Derrida's work as a 'general negative theology', see Owen Ware, "Impossible Passions: Derrida and Negative Theology," *Philosophy Today* 49:2/5 (2005), 171-183. See also, on this theme, Harold Coward and Toby Foshay, eds. *Derrida and Negative Theology*, Albany, NY: State University of New York Press, 1992.

to speak'.[17] Yet this, for him, is not something we can represent in any sense. Moreover, as he will make clear elsewhere, consciousness itself is inseparable from language and from representation, that is, from the establishment of the human subject over and against its animality.[18] The anthropologies that sustain these borders (Judeo-Christian theological ones at that) are therefore indeed themselves dependent upon the aporetic nature of our existence, the impossibility of our accurately describing what we are in-itself (in-ourselves).[19]

This is the first critique of the *as such*-ness that Derrida will mount (and this is the logic that will in turn frame the Derrida-Agamben debate). There may be something there, out beyond us, a presence lingering before us, but it is not something we can find a way to represent. For him, being responsible for the unrepresentable thing, the 'wholly other', who is always the other before us, means enduring the experience and condition (and, hence, limitations) of our aporetic existence, realizing only then that we are dependent upon language and inescapably bound to it.[20] In this state, we find the aporia of the *possible* impossible, the *impossible* possible, or the experience of possibility *as* impossibility. The attempt to experience this limit thus marks, for Derrida, the prominent rise of the *as such*, what everything can be said to wait for (its form of messianicity) as its potential appearance effaces the borders and boundaries upon which all of our representations rely.[21] The crossing of borders and boundaries, of course, and as this potential appearance points toward, is what defines an apophatic theology, precisely what Derrida does not wish to engage in as such because he believes it *cannot* be engaged with *as such*.[22] We must endure the aporia which

[17] Derrida, "How to Avoid Speaking," 166.

[18] Derrida, "How to Avoid Speaking," 156. See also, his remarks on animality in general in Jacques Derrida, *The Animal That Therefore I Am*, ed. Marie-Louis Mallet, trans. David Wills, New York: Fordham University Press, 2008, as well as Leonard Lawlor, *This Is Not Sufficient: An Essay on Animality and Human Nature in Derrida*, New York: Columbia University Press, 2007.

[19] Jacques Derrida, Aporias, trans. Thomas Dutoit, Stanford: Stanford University Press, 1993, 40-1.

[20] Derrida, *Aporias*, 16.

[21] Derrida, *Aporias*, 72-3.

[22] Derrida, "Sauf le nom," *On the Name*, ed. Thomas Dutoit, trans. David Wood, John P. Leavey, Jr. and Ian McLeod, Stanford: Stanford University Press, 1995, 36.

strictly speaking cannot be *endured as such*: 'the ultimate aporia is the impossibility of the aporia *as such*'.[23] There is no more originary path to take than this experience of the inexperienceable that must be endured, but not contorted into some form of presence. The event *as such* does not then itself appear because it is too monstrous; if it did appear, in fact, we would not be able to reason, or to think the future.[24] Negative theology, for its part, attempts to surpass the aporia which cannot be exceeded within reason, and Derrida, who is far too Kantian in this respect, cannot acknowledge any such possibility.[25]

This same relationship between the *as if* and the *as such* which Derrida here plays upon can be seen perhaps more clearly within his writings on the poetry of Paul Celan, a more than occasional subject of study for him, and for good reason, as I intend to show.[26] In the context of a series of lectures devoted to exploring the concept of sovereignty, Derrida contends that poetry portrays a certain (sovereign) sense of majesty through its language, yet it does not present what it attempts to present; it only bears witness to a presence that cannot be presented. As he puts it, 'Majesty is here majestic, and it is poetry, insofar as it bears witness to the present, the now, the "presence" of the human'.[27] Derrida himself, of course, would not favor this primacy of presence that Celan sought to establish within the majesty of the poem. He says as much immediately following his acknowledgement of how important this primacy to presence is to Celan. This is likewise in keeping with the Derrida, it should be said, who had launched numerous attacks on

---

[23] Derrida, *Aporias*, 78.

[24] Jacques Derrida, *Rogues: Two Essays on Reason*, trans. Pascale-Anne Brault and Michael Naas, Stanford: Stanford University Press, 2004, 144. On the Kantian legacy in Derrida's thought, see also Phil Rothfield, ed. *Kant After Derrida*, Manchester: Clinamen Press, 2002.

[25] Derrida, "Sauf le nom," 54.

[26] Cf. Gert-Jan van der Heiden, "The Poetic Experience of Language and the Task of Thinking: Derrida on Celan," *Philosophy Today* (2009), 115-125. For a reading of Derrida in relation to the poetry of Wallace Stevens, see J. Hillis Miller, "Anachronistic Reading," *Derrida Today* 3:1 (2010), 75-91.

[27] Derrida, *The Beast and the Sovereign*, 231. Cf. Derrida's remarks on majesty and sovereignty as they were initially published in his *Rogues*.

the 'metaphysics of presence' which attempts to posit itself as sovereign within the history of western thought.[28]

As he often put it, the poem, or poetics in fact, has a secret, in essence that it 'conceals itself by exhibiting its concealment *as such*'.[29] Yet it is a concealment that can only be 'shown' (as *only* being a concealment), which is to say, it does not show the content of the secret itself. And secrets, we are elsewhere told, are always involved in acts of representation, though they themselves cannot be represented.[30] Derrida will even venture out so far on this point to assert that the poetic work 'perhaps no longer derives from self-presentation *as such*', only from the exposure of what it is intent to conceal.[31] Hence, we are left to speculate as to how much presence, sacrality, revelation or religious desiring could even be present in our world, since all they could potentially testify to would be the absence of any genuine presence. How much of it indeed could *be* present since our (theo)-poetics no longer arises from a presumed presentation?[32]

What he seems, in fact, to be approaching at times is a poetic presence beyond the political present, a majesty of the event beyond the majesty of political power, a distinction with wider implications that Derrida only hints toward at times, or circles around as if indicating that there were something more there to be taken up. This would be

---

[28] Cf. his initial essays in *Writing and Difference*, trans. Alan Bass, Chicago: University of Chicago Press, 1978.

[29] Jacques Derrida, *Sovereignties in Question: The Poetics of Paul Celan*, eds. Thomas Dutoit and Outi Pasanen, New York: Fordham University Press, 2005, 95.

[30] Cf. Derrida, "How to Avoid Speaking," 156 and "Passions: An Oblique Offering," *On the Name*, 24-5. In the latter essay, he goes on to add that secrets are neither sacred nor profane, neither involved in a 'learned ignorance' (negative theology) nor an esoteric doctrine (mysticism) (26). See also, his remarks on the 'secret' in a series of interviews geared toward this thematic in Jacques Derrida and Maurizio Ferraris, *A Taste for the Secret*, eds. Giacomo Donis and David Webb, trans. Giacomo Donis, Cambridge: Polity, 2001, especially 58-9.

[31] Derrida, *Sovereignties in Question*, 96.

[32] On the merger of theology and poetics into a *theo*poetics, see the initial work of Amos Niven Wilder, *TheoPoetic: Theology and the Religious Imagination*, Philadelphia: Fortress, 1976, as well as its recent usage in the writings of Richard Kearney, *Anatheism: Returning to God After God*, New York: Columbia University Press, 2010, and John Caputo, *The Weakness of God: A Theology of the Event*, Bloomington, IN: Indiana University Press, 2006.

something that indeed opens up Derrida's own writing toward the poetic lineage that ranges from Stevens to Rich, and perhaps even to the critical analyses of Lacoue-Labarthe and Agamben, yet which also keeps him at a certain distance from them all, refusing to concede that there is anything beyond our representations that we can access *as such*.[33]

In Celan's work, Derrida discovers an approach to the event contained within poetry that is not an essence or an origin locatable within the poetic experience, as we have already seen.[34] There is a majesty of the present within the poetic that is sovereign, and that calls us to it; yet it is not a politically sovereign form as would befit a king, for example. It is a stepping outside of the human being that is, he says, proper to artistic (re)presentations, proper perhaps even for theological speculations.[35] It is no less than a division of those already existing political divisions, a double-division, or a division of division itself that poetry undertakes as an-*other* form of majesty.[36] Speaking of the two foreigners present in the poem, for example, a difference somewhat like the 'passage of poetry' which Celan identifies as possible for humanity to see beyond itself, Derrida draws upon the difference between them in order to attempt to locate something of the present event within the poetic. As he puts it,

---

[33] On his distinguishing himself from the work of Agamben, see his remarks on him made in the same lectures on *The Beast and the Sovereign*, 92f and 313f. On his proximity and yet distance from Lacoue-Labarthe, see his introduction to the latter's *Typology: Mimesis, Philosophy, Politics*, trans. Christopher Fynsk, Stanford: Stanford University Press, 1998, entitled 'Desistance'.

[34] Derrida, *The Beast and the Sovereign*, 267.

[35] Derrida, *The Beast and the Sovereign*, 260. Malek Moazzam-Doulat, for example, has suggested that Derrida's messianism actually serves to reveal a god who must either hide or recede and is therefore not sovereign. Cf. Malek Moazzam-Doulat, "Future Impossible: Carl Schmitt, Jacques Derrida, and the Problem of Political Messianism," *Philosophy Today* (2008), 73-81.

[36] This same 'double division' which Derrida speaks of is developed in much further detail and in a somewhat parallel register by Giorgio Agamben in his *The Time that Remains: A Commentary on the Letter to the Romans*, trans. Patricia Dailey, Stanford: Stanford University Press, 2005. Despite Agamben's insistence that his approach is in stark contrast to Derrida's, their mutual illumination of the poetic in regard to sovereignty strikes a similar chord.

> This is the difference, in the punctuality of the now, in the pinpoint of the present moment, of *my* present, between *on the one hand*, my other living present (retained or anticipated by an indispensable movement of retention and pretension), and, *on the other hand*, wholly other, the present of the other the temporality of which cannot be reduced, included, assimilated, introjected, appropriated into mine, cannot even resemble it or be similar to it, a present or proper time of the other that I must surely let go, radically giving it up, but also the very possibility of which (the *perhaps* beyond all knowledge) is the chance both of the encounter (*Begegnung*) and of this event, this advent, of what is called poetry. An improbable poetry ("who knows") but a poetry to take one's breath away and turn it, and so also turn life and path, which can still be a path of art both wider and narrower.[37]

An 'improbable poetry' that yet contains the ability to 'take one's breath away and turn it', which appears then to have a real bearing upon how we define, or *cease to define* ourselves within this space. Yet this, according to him, is done without an actual presence of the other being presented. It is somehow, structurally, a part of our struggle with the 'wholly other' before us, an openness that must be maintained seemingly to 'openness' itself. This is to keep us 'present' to ourselves then, to that which is always beyond us, always singular, always an event at the heart of those aporias which constantly define and yet elude us.

In so many words, this is what he will speak of elsewhere as an *envoi* that is foreign to representation and is yet not exactly gathered under the label of presence either. It is a 'pre-ontological' sending that does not gather itself at all under any singular heading; it is rather gathered only through its dividing of itself, an act that occurs within itself and not at the presentation of an 'other' (a presence) from without. As he puts it in this context, there is nothing present before it as it is only 'the other in itself without itself', an act of carrying the other before us

[37] Derrida, *The Beast and the Sovereign*, 271-2.

without affixing identity to either them or us.[38] Perhaps then there is a presentation beyond representation that lurks underneath his work on language, undergirding its strength and not so far off in the end from other attempts to locate a presence seemingly beyond us. As Derrida indicates within his earlier remarks on Celan, there is ultimately a *poetic* revolution possible within the *political* revolution, a revolution within the living present that is also a 'dethroning of majesty' which goes beyond all forms of knowledge.[39] As we had previously been told, there is a faith in poetry that is a faith in God, a present faith itself present in the majesty of the poem.[40]

4. Conclusion

How are we to define the presence that cannot be present outside of our regulative ideals, but only 'present' in the aporetic openings that must be cultivated within? Is this what the many poetic and mystical traditions have actually sought to present to us over the centuries, a presentation of the aporia itself, a presence not of the divine because not beyond the self but one entirely given within? For Derrida, this is a messianic event that will not end with some determinate content (an historical *messianism*); it is rather part of the structure of the system of representations itself. This is ultimately what allows Derrida to summon Celan once again in yet another context as he who bears witness to the opening of multiple 'other' poetics without end that are furthered through this reality.[41]

In this opening, perhaps somewhat akin to Rilke's notion of *the Open* as poetically formulated in his *Dunio Elegies*, we are witness to the profound mystical configuration of the self, a potential form of mysticism that cannot be easily comprehended or codified, but which yet works according to a regulative logic of the aporia. This is a radical openness that never dies away or tones itself down, but which, rather, constantly opens itself up to the event before us, and yet also within

[38] Cf. Jacques Derrida, "Envoi," *Psyche: Inventions of the Other*, Vol. I, eds. Peggy Kamuf and Elizabeth Rottenberg, Stanford: Stanford University Press, 2007, 127. See also his remarks on a possible 'preorigin' in his essay "Khōra," *On the Name*, 126.

[39] Derrida, *The Beast and the Sovereign*, 273.

[40] Derrida, *The Beast and the Sovereign*, 230

[41] Jacques Derrida, Monolinguism *of the Other; or, The Prosthesis of Origin*, trans. Patrick Mensah, Stanford: Stanford University Press, 1998.

us. In the end, and I offer this as a conclusion, what I perhaps hear here are the echoes of a presence resonating from within, something just barely out of reach, just barely divine, just barely a glimpse of what truth must continue to unwind down the slow, graceful turnings that take place within the animal who is immersed in language. This is the frame through which we might just begin to see the mystical arise. And so, perhaps Rich puts it best when she, the one who dives after the wreck as the 'thing itself', tells us that she too struggles to break free from language, but that she nonetheless finds something powerful, and true, within language:

> If from time to time I envy
> the pure annunciations to the eye
> the *visio beatifica*
> if from time to time I long to turn [...]
> for return to the concrete and everlasting world
> what in fact I keep choosing
> are these words, these whispers, conversations
> from which time after time the truth breaks moist and green.[42]

References

01. Agamben, Giorgio, *Infancy and History: On the Destruction of Experience*, trans. Liz Heron, London: Verso, 1993.
02. Agamben, Giorgio, *Potentialities: Collected Essays in Philosophy*, trans. Daniel Heller-Roazen, Stanford: Stanford University Press, 2000.
03. Agamben, Giorgio, *The Time that Remains: A Commentary on the Letter to the Romans*, trans. Patricia Dailey, Stanford: Stanford University Press, 2005.
04. Bigger, Charles P., Between Chora *and the* Good*: Metaphor's Metaphysical Neighborhood*, New York: Fordham University Press, 2005.
05. Caputo, John, *The Weakness of God: A Theology of the Event*, Bloomington, IN: Indiana University Press, 2006.

[42] Adrienne Rich, "Cartographies of Silence," The *Dream of a Common Language: Poems 1974-1977*, New York: W.W. Norton, 1978. This same impulse can be seen on display in her series of poems entitled "Contradictions: Tracking Poems," *Your Native Land, Your Life*, New York: W.W. Norton, 1986.

06. Coward, Harold and Toby Foshay, eds. *Derrida and Negative Theology*, Albany, NY: State University of New York Press, 1992.
07. Critchley, Simon, *Things Merely Are: Philosophy in the Poetry of Wallace Stevens*, London: Routledge, 2005.
08. Derrida, Jacques, *Writing and Difference*, trans. Alan Bass, Chicago: University of Chicago Press, 1978.
09. Derrida, Jacques, Aporias, trans. Thomas Dutoit, Stanford: Stanford University Press, 1993.
10. Derrida, Jacques, *On the Name*, ed. Thomas Dutoit, trans. David Wood, John P. Leavey, Jr. and Ian McLeod, Stanford: Stanford University Press, 1995.
11. Derrida, Jacques, *Monolinguism of the Other; or, The Prosthesis of Origin*, trans. Patrick Mensah, Stanford: Stanford University Press, 1998.
12. Derrida, Jacques, *Rogues: Two Essays on Reason*, trans. Pascale-Anne Brault and Michael Naas, Stanford: Stanford University Press, 2004.
13. Derrida, Jacques, *Sovereignties in Question: The Poetics of Paul Celan*, eds. Thomas Dutoit and Outi Pasanen, New York: Fordham University Press, 2005.
14. Derrida, Jacques, "Envoi," *Psyche: Inventions of the Other*, Vol. I, eds. Peggy Kamuf and Elizabeth Rottenberg, Stanford: Stanford University Press, 2007.
15. Derrida, Jacques, "How to Avoid Speaking: Denials," *Psyche: Inventions of the Other*, Vol. II, eds. Peggy Kamuf and Elizabeth Rottenberg, Stanford: Stanford University Press, 2008.
16. Derrida, Jacques, *The Animal That Therefore I Am*, ed. Marie-Louis Mallet, trans. David Wills, New York: Fordham University Press, 2008.
17. Derrida, Jacques, *The Beast and the Sovereign*, eds. Michel Lisse, Marie-Louise Mallet and Ginette Michaud, trans. Geoffrey Bennington, Chicago: University of Chicago Press, 2009.
18. Derrida, Jacques and Maurizio Ferraris, *A Taste for the Secret*, eds. Giacomo Donis and David Webb, trans. Giacomo Donis, Cambridge: Polity, 2001.
19. Estrin, Barbara L., "Space-Off and Voice-Over: Adrienne Rich and Wallace Stevens," *Women's Studies* 25 (1995) 23-46.
20. Hart, Kevin, *The Trespass of the Sign: Deconstruction, Theology and Philosophy*, Cambridge: Cambridge University Press, 1989.
21. Hedley, Jane, "Surviving to Speak New Language: Mary Daly and Adrienne Rich," *Hypatia* 7:2 (1992) 40-62.
22. van der Heiden, Gert-Jan, "The Poetic Experience of Language and the Task of Thinking: Derrida on Celan," *Philosophy Today* (2009) 115-125.
23. Kant, Immanuel, *Critique of Pure Reason*, eds. and trans. Paul Guyer and Allen W. Wood, Cambridge: Cambridge University Press, 1997.
24. Kant, Immanuel, *Lectures on Logic*, trans. J. Michael Young, Cambridge: Cambridge University Press, 2004.

25. Kearney, Richard, *Anatheism: Returning to God After God*, New York: Columbia University Press, 2010.
26. Kessler, Michael and Christian Sheppard, eds. *Mystics: Presence and Aporia*, Chicago: University of Chicago Press, 2003.
27. Lacoue-Labarthe, Philippe, *Typology: Mimesis, Philosophy, Politics*, trans. Christopher Fynsk, Stanford: Stanford University Press, 1998.
28. Lacoue-Labarthe, Philippe, *Poetry as Experience*, trans. Andrea Tarnowski, Stanford: Stanford University Press, 1999.
29. Lawlor, Leonard, *This Is Not Sufficient: An Essay on Animality and Human Nature in Derrida*, New York: Columbia University Press, 2007.
30. Marion, Jean-Luc, *Being Given: Toward a Phenomenology of Givenness*, trans. Jeffrey Kosky, Stanford: Stanford University Press, 2002.
31. Martis, John, *Philippe Lacoue-Labarthe: Representation and the Loss of the Subject*, New York: Fordham University Press, 2005.
32. Miller, J. Hillis, "Anachronistic Reading," Derrida *Today* 3:1 (2010) 75-91.
33. Moazzam-Doulat, Malek, "Future Impossible: Carl Schmitt, Jacques Derrida, and the Problem of Political Messianism," *Philosophy Today* (2008) 73-81.
34. Rich, Adrienne, *The Will to Change: Poems 1968-1970*, New York: W.W. Norton, 1971.
35. Rich, Adrienne, *Diving into the Wreck: Poems 1971-1972*, New York: W.W. Norton, 1973.
36. Rich, Adrienne, *The Dream of a Common Language: Poems 1974-1977*, New York: W.W. Norton, 1978.
37. Rich, Adrienne, *Your Native Land, Your Life*, New York: W.W. Norton, 1986.
38. Rich, Adrienne, *An Atlas of the Difficult World: Poems 1988-1991*, New York: W.W. Norton, 1991.
39. Rich, Adrienne, *What Is Found There: Notebooks on Poetry and Politics*, New York: W.W. Norton, 2003.
40. Ross, Alison, *The Aesthetic Paths of Philosophy: Presentation in Kant, Heidegger, Lacoue-Labarthe, and Nancy*, Stanford: Stanford University Press, 2007.
41. Phil Rothfield, ed. *Kant After Derrida*, Manchester: Clinamen Press, 2002.
42. Stevens, Wallace, *Collected Poetry and Prose*, New York: Library of America, 1997.
43. Vaihinger, Hans, *The Philosophy of As If: A System of the Theoretical, Practical, and Religious Fictions of Mankind*, trans. C.K. Ogden, London: Routledge, 1965.
44. Ware, Owen, "Impossible Passions: Derrida and Negative Theology," *Philosophy Today* 49:2/5 (2005) 171-183.
45. Wilder, Amos Niven, *TheoPoetic: Theology and the Religious Imagination*, Philadelphia: Fortress, 1976.

6

Identifying the Mystical in Literature
Space versus Place in the Works of Willa Cather

Ms. Elisabeth Bayley
Katholieke Universiteit Leuven, Belgium

> "There are pleasure gardens in the world as well as graveyards, waltzes as well as funeral marches, living men as well as dead, young women as well as old, sonnets as well as epitaphs."
> (Willa Cather)[1]

> "Place is not background, as in the Holbein woodcuts, but the subject of meditation." (Judith Fryer)[2]

The American early 20th Century author Willa Cather uses images to string together places within the imagination of her readers. She takes objects and describes their 'livelihoods', thereby giving her characters experiences which guide the recesses of readers' minds to a multitude of places they might not have previously felt or experienced in their own lives. Her ability to use ordinary characters' lives, objects and places within her work, and to depict them with such a craft that is uniquely her own, gives way to experiences which appear as realities within her fictional stories and which also serve to bring the reader into a realm

---

[1] Bernice Slote, ed. *The Kingdom of Art: Willa Cather's First Principles and Critical Statements 1893-1896*, Lincoln: University of Nebraska Press, 1966, 341.

[2] Judith Fryer, *Felicitous Space: The imaginative Structures of Edith Wharton and Willa Cather*, Chapel Hill, NC: The University of North Carolina Press, 1986, 315.

of the imagination. The ability to write the way Cather did was a truly poetic venture. It is this avenue of the imagination, which Cather walks her readers down, that I am going to explore in this paper. Furthermore, I will look at the ways in which her skill at producing a process of poetic enlightenment creates a space for a spiritual or mystical experience of liminality and potentiality.

1. Space versus Place

Historically, *space* has taken center stage over *place*. Space has been understood as infinite and place as a compartmentalized concept that took shape within space.[3] It is only recently that place has taken a more prominent position. The most current phase in this conception of space has no clearly delineated lines of definition. "...Depending on the author one happens to be reading, it may connote logical coherence, practical consistency, self-regulation and the relations of the parts to the whole, the engendering of like by like in a set of places, the logic of container *versus* contents, and so on. We are forever hearing about the space of this and/or the space of that [...]" (Lefebvre 3). Lefebvre's perspective is that space has become a much broader concept than the traditional understanding of it found within the history of its meaning. It now includes the philosophical constructions that consist of a more individualized understanding of space, one that is located within one's own mental perceptions and placement of experiences. This understanding brings about a different conception of space and allots for place to come to the forefront of thought.

Thus, place is constituted more recently, as something which Edward S. Casey, in his book *The Fate of Place: A Philosophical History,* points out as:

[3] From the time of Aristotle, space took on a classification category for the senses and moved with Descartes to "the realm of the absolute". From there it was with Kant that "realm of consciousness" took over the understanding of space, which meant that it was a "transcendental and essentially ungraspable" structure. Out of this Kantian understanding of space (combined with the entrance of the mathematical exploration of space) arose the idea that space is more of a "mental thing" or "mental place" (Lefebvre 1-3).

> [...] considered with regard to living organisms and, in particular, the lived human body. Not only does this put us in a better position to account for the specifically human experience of place; it open up fresh vistas on place itself—allowing us to grasp its scope as well as its limits—while eliciting a renewed interest in the specificities of implacement, which had become submerged under the twin modern obsessions with infinite Space and chronometric Time. The seemingly contracted locus of the lived body, which is always just *here*, has proved to be an effective basis for what has become an expansive vision of what place is all about, even when it is located over *there* and far away. (332)

In Casey's historical look at place, space has become a concept that is located in the place of the body, the physicality of the 'lived human body.' Thus, space is then understood as something that is founded in a place versus the previously historically conceived notion of a place as grounded in space.[4]

It is out of these two conceptions of space and place that Cather's work might be looked at through the theoretical lens of Gaston Bachelard. Bachelard's well-known work *The Poetics of Space* explores the way in which poetry serves to produce or invoke a grid of constituted points from memory and experience, that is, within one's self, in order to open oneself up to a greater immensity. Bachelard locates space as a configuration of our previous experiences and he sees that these are what constitute the current reality of the everyday. He therefore sees the work of the poet as one of great importance in that their words are able to awaken a "stage setting" of one's past and allow one to enter into the space of "compressed time."[5] In his work, he therefore uses images that he argues maintain the space of our inner-world.

---

[4] See Luce Irigaray, "Place, Interval: A reading of Aristotle, *Physics IV*," in *An Ethics of Sexual Difference*, trans. C. Burke and G.C. Gill, Ithaca: Cornell University Press, 1993.

[5] Bachelard believes that a "topoanalysis" takes place within the poetic space. He writes that, "[...] the systematic psychological study of the sites of our intimate lives. In the theater of the past that is constituted by memory, the stage setting maintains that characters in their dominant roles. At times we think we know ourselves in time, when

Willa Cather is an exceptional pictorialist. She can paint a verbal image that sticks to one's gut while yet growing from there into multiple meanings. This is the gift of Cather as an author. It is this ability of Cather's that invokes and makes great use of our sense for poetic space, or as Gaston Bachelard writes, "The great function of poetry is to give us back the situations of our dreams" (15) and that, "[...] we should not forget that these dream values communicate poetically from soul to soul. To read poetry is essentially to daydream" (17). Cather invokes 'one's dreams' or daydreams, as Bachelard calls them, even if she is not writing in a traditional poetic style.[6] Her work, however, does hold poetic qualities that are depicted through the use of images similar to the images that Bachelard himself points out in his book as being poetic. It is, however, important to note that Bachelard does not believe that the poetic image is subject to an "inner thrust" nor that it is an "echo of the past" but that "[...] through the brilliance of an image, the distant past resounds with echoes, and it is hard to know at what depth these echoes will reverberate and die away. Because of its novelty and its action, the poetic image has an entity and a dynamism of its own; it is referable to a direct *ontology*" (xvi). Thus, we will now begin to look at the ways in which Cather's work produces poetic images.

2. Cather's Poetic Space

Let us begin by looking at the use of the home or house within Cather's work. The house is what Bachelard understands as one of the foundations within the imagination, and accordingly Cather creates a poetic space within the houses she depicts in her novels that form a foundation for the reader's imagination to latch onto. To name just a few examples of this, in Alexandra's house in *O Pioneers!* it is described as "curiously

all we know is a sequence of fixations in the spaces of the being's stability—a being who does not want to melt away, and who, even in the past, when he sets out in search of things past, wants time to 'suspend' its flight. In its countless alveoli space contains compressed time. That is what space is for" (Bachelard 8).

[6] "'I can't write plots', she [Cather] said once. 'Sometimes I wish I could, but we have to do with what we have. I don't see life in terms of action. Persons like me who see it in terms of thought and imagery would best keep away from suspense. It's design they want, not conflict'" (Hoover 135). For further reading of Cather's poetry see, Willa Cather, *April Twilights*, Gloucestershire, UK: Dodo Press, 2008.

unfinished and uneven in comfort" (42), and she goes on to describe her house as a mixture of old things from her childhood log cabin home and rooms that are just barely furnished. Here, Cather uses the poetic imagery of the house, in its tension of full and empty, sparse and decorated. Another example is the image of Jim Burden grandparent's house that Cather gives in *My Antonia* as one with a kitchen filled with smells of cookies, cleanliness, comforts and sunlight and where 'Jimmy' can take a hot bath (502). Through these images, the house is given the picture of comfort and safety. Or in *A Lost Lady* Cather gives the description of the Forrester's house as odd, with sloping roofs, too narrow porches and fragile pillars (4). Here the picture of a house is one with awkward dimensions and a great deal of instability. The descriptive sense of houses is present in most of Cather's stories[7] and serves in this sense to create a foundation for the reader's receptiveness to the consequent narrative.

Cather seems indeed to be drawing upon the same fundamental insight that Bachelard points out when he states that:

> Thought and experience are not the only things that sanction human values. The values that belong to daydreaming mark humanity in its depths. Daydreaming even has a privilege of autovalorization. It derives direct pleasure from its own being. Therefore, the places in which we have *experienced daydreaming* reconstitute themselves in a new daydream, and it is because our memories of former dwelling-places are relived as daydreams that these dwelling-places of the past remain in us for all time. (6)

---

[7] For example, the description of the kitchen in *Shadows on the Rock* creates a sense of warmth, where "[…] there was a small, low-roofed kitchen, built of stone, through the house itself was built of wood in the earliest Quebec manner, double walls, with sawdust and ashes filling the space between the two frames, making a protection nearly four feet thick against the winter cold" (Cather, *Shadows on the Rock*, 14). Or the depiction of the house that Claude Wheeler builds in *One of Ours* where it is described as "in perfect order" by his wife, Enid, but is at the same time, untouchable in its pristine attributes and thus, unlivable (which is a foreshadowing to Claude moving out of it in the end) (Cather, *One of Ours*, 280).

Through Cather's use of the description of houses, she is able to create a poetic space where the reader's daydreaming of the past images of houses is able to reverberate with her images of homes. When one imagines or daydreams a home one always contemplates a mingling of houses from the past or the places where previous daydreams took place, and these places are echoed within any subsequent daydreams. Thus, "the house is one of the greatest powers of integration for the thoughts, memories and dreams of mankind" (Bachelard 6) and Cather uses the image of the house within her novels to create the reverberations of past images with the presently depicted homes of her novels.[8]

Bachelard considers the image of the house as a foundation for daydreaming and uses different elements within the home to describe different poetic spaces which illuminate daydreaming and create concrete psychical places.[9] Cather likewise uses multiple images within her novels in her descriptions of different aspects of the home to create a stream of daydreaming for her reader. Once again, by looking at her novels, this can be seen in Bartley Alexander's house, for example, where he "stood six feet and more in the archway, glowing with strength and cordiality [...]"(5), an image which served to make the archway of the house seem to be similar to Bartley's being the pillar of his house and his family. Another example can be found in *The Song of the Lark*, when Thea gets enough money to decorate and make her own room. Cather places meaning in everything that Thea does to decorate and add to her room. She tells the reader about the curtains, wallpaper, the dresser and the mirror, giving individual meaning to each of these items. But more importantly, Cather sets Thea up in the attic where she could "live a double life" (191), one during the day with her family and one at

[8] "First, 'home' stands for the fact that we persistently need a location where we can pass through the stages of life and become the person we are potentially. Second, we need a place where we can belong to a community. Third, we need a place that offers a fruitful relationship with the natural elements, with plants and animals and with the rhythms of the season. Finally, we need a place that offers access to the sacred (however we understand that term)—perhaps, crucially, relates us to *life itself as sacred*" (Sheldrake 10).

[9] Edward S. Casey writes concerning Bachelard "[...] that there is a valid sense of place for nonsensible items; place can be nonphysical and yet still count fully as place" and "It is evident to Bachelard, however, that poetic images flare up *somewhere*, and the place in which they do so is psychical in nature" (Casey 288).

night where she could be alone in her room. The depiction of St. Peter in *The Professor's House* is yet another example of this. Cather tells the story of St. Peter in his office in the attic after the rest of his family had moved out of the house. She writes "[...] his hand went resolutely up two flights of stairs to the third floor where, under the slope of the mansard roof, there was one room still furnished—that is, if it had ever been furnished"(16). In these three examples, Cather uses alternating conceptual constructs within the structure of the home to create an image of reaching upward. Even the attic is used as an image where "[...] fears are easily 'rationalized' [and how] in the attic, the day's experiences can always efface the fears of night" (Bachelard 19). Cather creates a sense of security in the reaching upward of space and structures within her novels, and unleashes a sense of security found in the upper areas of the house,[10] versus the use of the cellar or the cave found, for example, in the description of the cave like home of the Shimerda's first home, in *My Antonia* (509).[11] The daydreaming of the mind is once again called forth to resound with Cather's poetic images that she situates within the home.

As we have seen, Cather is able to render the reader a daydreamer with her poetic use of images of the home and the spaces within the home, such as the attic. But what Cather is known for is her use of descriptions of the land. Bachelard writes:

> Faced with a quiet world, on a soothing plain, mankind can enjoy peace and repose. But in an imagined world, the sights of the plain often produce only the most commonplace effects. To restore their action to these sights, it is therefore necessary to supply a new image. An unexpected literary image can so move the spirit that it will follow the induction of tranquility. In fact, the literary image can make the spirit sufficiently sensitive to receive unbelievably fine impressions. (208)

[10] Cather portrays the use of the attic as a safe place in *Sapphira and the Slave Girl*. She has Mrs. Blake's children upstairs in their "sick beds" and Cather uses this image to provoke a sense of security for their lives. However, in this imagery she invokes a unique mixture of death with the sense of security in the upper regions of the house (Cather, *Sapphira and the Slave Girl*, 259-60).

[11] Or, the cave scene in Cather, *Death Comes for the Archbishop*, 127.

Cather is a master at producing "unexpected literary image[s]" which can move the reader into a place of "tranquility". This can be seen in *Shadows on the Rock* when Cécile was coming back from her visit to the Pigeon household with Pierre, Cécile is comforted by the sight of the "[...] rock of Kebec and the sun on the slate roofs" (225) sticking out on the shoreline. She also does this in *Death Comes for the Archbishop* where Bishop Latour is lost in the desert and the land looks repetitive and he happens upon a juniper tree in the shape of a cross (18). Or, of course, one of Cather's most famous images is the unexpected image in *My Antonia* where she describes the plough that had been left standing in a field. She writes: "There it was, heroic in size, a picture writing on the sun" (622). Cather thus uses the unexpected in her descriptions of the landscape because she seems to sense the important poetic use of the image and likewise the way it can draw in one's imagination. Sheldrake points out that "Apart from human embodiment the most common experience of place, or being placed, involves familiar landscapes. Any analysis of place inevitably has a subjective element. People learn to be who they are by relating to the foundational landscapes of childhood or to adopted landscapes that became significant because of later events and associations. Familiar landscapes are the geography of human imagination" (14). Because some of the landscapes that Cather described in her writings were not always known to her readers, she uses the imagery of ordinary objects within barren landscapes to create a unique image within the imagination.[12] Moreover, Cather knew that landscapes played an important part within her literature and how her depictions of them could create a large poetic awakening within her readers.[13]

---

[12] For further exploration of the connection between Cather's writing and the imagination see Judith Fryer, *Felicitous Space*, where she writes, "Center implies circumference, a place in space. To find the center of one's boundless desire, to give it form, is to begin in a space that is felicitous, one that frees the imagination" (Fryer, 293).

[13] As Simon Schama points out, "Landscapes are culture before they are nature; constructs of the imagination projected onto wood and water and rock" (Schama. 610). Cather understood this notion and even writes about it in *O Pioneers!* "Of all the bewildering things about a new country, the absence of human landmarks is one of the most depressing and disheartening" (Cather, *O Pioneers!* in *Willa Cather: Three Novels*, 13-14).

3. Place as 'Mystical'

Can this reverberating of the imagination through poetic images truly be understood as the experiencing of place however? Casey points out that the location of place is difficult to define or locate but that the reason it is, is because it can be discussed as existing in a multitude of places. Casey writes that "The new basis of any putative primacy of place are themselves multiple: bodily certainly, but also psychical, nomadological, architectural, institutional, and sexual. Since there is no single basis of the primacy of place, there is no monolithic foundation on which this primacy could be built. What is at stake is a polyvalent primacy—an equiprimoridality of primary terms" (337). Within Casey's historical analysis of place, it could be argued that yes, there is a place that exists within the poetic echoing of imagination and that it would fall under the "psychical". Furthermore, within Cather's work, and through the theoretical lens of Bachclard, onc might see that there is a place within the body where the imagination becomes the identification of place through poetic images. Bachelard writes that, "Contrary to metaphor, we can devote our reading being to an image, since it confers being upon us. In fact, the image, which is the pure product of absolute imagination, is a phenomenon of being; it is also one of the specific phenomena of the speaking creature" (75). The images that Cather invokes in the imagination are located in the "phenomenon of being" and, therefore, they find their locus in the body and place of our psychical processes. Thus, there can be a poetic space within the place of the imagination that is yet located in the place of the body.

Considering that we have identified a psychical place within the body we now can look at an understanding of place for the body as a whole. A helpful understanding of our bodies can be found in the work of Luce Irigaray, for example. She in fact founds her understanding of place as a physical reality found within the body. She writes, "The universe contains all bodies. The sky, the air, the earth are containers that are not specific to each of us (male or female). But each of us (male or female) has a place—this place that envelops only his or her body, the first envelope of our bodies, the corporeal identity, the boundary, that which delineates us from other bodies" (36). A binary understanding of the body is what Irigaray moves away from.[14] She sees the body like an "envelope" that simultaneously contains and spills out. Philip Leonard points out that "Irigaray extrapolates from the binary framework of presence and absence, self and other, masculine and feminine, a liminal and interstitial 'woman as lover' who is neither inside nor outside sexual order" (148). She therefore sees the body as something which moves from a binary framework to a more "interstitial" space of the body that is neither in nor out. This understanding sees that the body is both a "container", which needs to be understood as the delineation of our own bodies from other bodies, and at the same time, an open "envelope". Thus, the body, in Irigaray's viewpoint is something that shifts and is no longer stagnant between the binary poles of the enveloped and the one who is an envelope.[15]

What happens when we think of the psychical aspects of the imagination in terms of how Irigaray understands the body as liminal? The imagination itself can certainly be seen as a liminal space in its own right, in constant flux because that is how the imagination works, setting forth images and daydreams that are not structured in time but free to roam about *with* time and with all detail becoming flexible to one's own imaginary constructs. However, echoing off this use of our imagination, poetic images therefore find a place within the body. In the fluid movement or "interstitial space" of the imagination, the place of the poetic image takes root in an ever moving and shifting limbo between fixed and fluid. Paolo Bartoloni has looked at the idea of literature as being interstitial in just such a way. As he writes, "Literature does not have the function of seducing and alluring the reader into a fantastic dimension disguised as reality. On the contrary it ought to disquiet, annoy and frustrate the

---

[14] Susan Rosowski writes: "These, then, were Cather's first principles—duality of two worlds and two selves, salvation through the imagination, exaltation of the artist-priest who can create living art, appreciation of the gift of sympathy" (Rosowski 10). Even though Cather might have perceived the world in a duality of sorts, she believed in the act of the imagination serving as some sort of salvation by creating a living art. Thus, her perceptions of duality might be better understood as more fluid in the light of the imagination.

[15] See Luce Irigaray, *An Ethics of Sexual Difference*, trans. Carolyn Burke and Gillian C. Gill, New York: Cornell University Press, 1984. 83-94. Here she points out that male wants to be enveloped while the female is the one who is the envelope.

reader, provoking him or her to react strongly, not in half-slumber, to the acrobatic, disjointed, zigzagging, ultimately heuristic writing whose function is not to represent but to travel and explore the interstice" (41). This interstice is the place that Giorgio Agamben, from whom Bartoloni draws upon, locates as the place of pure potentiality within us. As Agamben himself writes, "For everyone a moment comes in which she or he must utter this 'I can,' which does not refer to any certainty or specific capacity but is, nevertheless, absolutely demanding. Beyond all faculties, this 'I can' does not mean anything—yet it marks what is, for each of us, perhaps the hardest and bitterest experience possible: the experience of potentiality" (178). Thus, here we see the place located in the psychical that through the poetic imagination creates a space that is interstitial, or a potential for an individual to say "I can", that is, to develop their inner world from the foundations of their "house" up into another reality. This daydreaming that is invoked by the poetic ends up bringing into the imagination different and alternative constructs of reality that are the result of an inclusion of sorts, of things that were previously not in the reader's imagination.[16]

4. Place as Political

We have thus located a place within the body and the imagination where a space exists of potentiality, something which Cather demonstrated quite adeptly in her novels. If we delve further into the ways in which relationships between the poetic space of the author and the daydreaming of the reader take place it is possible to understand that this is in itself a very political position. The potentiality of the interstitial space, the in-between, or the possible, is political in and of itself in that it refuses to put itself into binary form but rather functions outside the realm of those understood (polarized) norms: in or out, black or white.[17] However,

[16] "'Mysticism' is taken [in a psychoanalytic bias] to mean any fusion of the subject and object into a greater whole that would result in psychic integration. If we add that any such integration is imaginary, we come close to Freud's description of the religious impulse in general as an 'oceanic feeling'" (Quance 84). On the connection between Agamben's work and mysticism see, Colby Dickinson, *Agamben and Theology*, London: T&T Clark, 2011.

[17] Agamben himself speaks against the formation of binary logics which have dominated over western thought for centuries. See Giorgio Agamben, 'What Is a Paradigm?' in

Michel de Certeau, in his seminal work *The Practice of Everyday Life*, looks at the idea of relation and writes that, "Analysis shows that a relation (always social) determines its terms, and not the reverse, and that each individual is a locus in which an incoherent (and often contradictory) plurality of such relational determinations interact" (xi). Thus, if the relations that one already has within the self are socially based, then how does one understand that there is a potentiality for different relations other than the binary?

When looking at Cather's work, we can then see that the relationships she draws between her homes, objects, landscapes and people are ones that she depicts through an understanding of the social relationship that is already in existence and which defines these terms. However, when she writes about the home and how a character might be like the home or when she writes about the landscapes and how the landscape was defined by the multi-ethnic groups of people moving onto the land,[18] or when her characters do not fit into the pre-inscribed norms of gender,[19] or even in her use of names,[20] she uses already pre-determined relations that are put in place by the existing norms of sociality and yet gives them unique descriptions over and beyond what has been ascribed to them. Here, Cather gives poetic space to relationships of sociality which reverberate off of and away from the already conceived notions of social place, challenging instead those concepts of the political found within common notions of property, community, gender and religion. She uses the understood poetic space then that Bachelard describes in order to expand them to include notions of relation that could cause one to be politically stirred from within due to the play between old relations with

The Signature of All Things: On Method, trans. Luca di Santo and Kevin Atell, New York: Zone, 2009.

[18] A few examples of this can be seen in Cather's description of converging cultures in *My Antonia*, *Death Comes for the Archbishop* or *O Pioneers!*

[19] For a few of the many examples of Cather's depictions of characters that question normally prescribed notions of gender, see her works containing the following characters: Alexandra Bergson and Ivar in *O Pioneers!*, or Thea Krohnberg in *The Song of the Lark*. Sandra M. Gilbert and Susan Gubar note that, "For her [Cather], the west is a place in which women at least briefly experienced an exhilarating autonomy" (Gilbert and Gubar 187).

[20] For further discussion on the use of names within Cather's work, see Butler 143-166.

the new. Thus, Cather's work not only gives way to poetic space within the place of imagination, but invokes the interstitial space of potentiality within her readers by creating poetic spaces within her fiction that call forth previously held social relations and yet alters them substantially, in accord with the limitless potential of each reader's imagination.

5. Conclusion

When looking at the place of the imagination within the body, and by locating the interstitial reality of the body and the imagination within the body, it becomes an incredibly powerful insight simply to understand this place of being in-between as creating a space of great potentiality for the reader to come and identify themselves over and beyond the social constructs before them. Once more, turning to Agamben, William Watkin writes, "The presence of an absence for Agamben is the true definition of potentiality, not the assumed movement from potentiality to actuality which we might call 'creation' or 'invention,' but the chance that potential will remain solely potential—potential inaction, in-creation, non-invention" (64).[21] In a word, that it could remain "fiction" and yet express the truth potentially forever. Thus, we see here that the ability of literature is not to unleash or unlock a definitive per se, but to open up what alrcady cxists within the creative imagination: the interstitial space of potentiality. After all, there will always be an "absence" in literature, because it is a work of fiction and bound within language, which in itself, is incomplete. "But it is precisely this incompleteness and its redistribution within the context of fiction and away from the referentiality of phenomena that fictive language can achieve the encounter with 'invisibility', can indeed become the 'invisible'" (Bartoloni 6).[22] Cather appears to understand this potentiality within the creative imagination in profound ways. She invokes it in

---

[21] Watkin continues, "Thus when Agamben goes on to define the artist, 'in this sense, we say of the architect that he or she has the *potential* to build, of the poet that he or she has the *potential* to write poems,' the actual and surprising definition of poetic being is the possession of faculty and not using it" (Watkin 64).

[22] "In medieval times, the notional 'gap' between presence and representation in both spoken and written language was conceived of, philosophically, as a consequence of the Fall" (Davis 111).

her readers by using poetic imagery that reverberates with the already created foundations within her readers' daydreams, something which could be understood as giving rise to a questioning of the politically socially given relations within the imagination.[23] Her creative use of houses and spaces within households, her use of landscapes mixed with objects and her ability to give significance to ordinary objects all open up the world of the imagination in order to invoke a potentiality within her readers. The presence of potentiality, invoked by imagination within poetic space, creates a place within the body that is ever in flux and in-between definitive points. And, as Cather does this, one might wonder, how can this place of interstitiality be named? Or *should* it even be named? I believe it is best described (though yet not named) by Cather's famous discussion regarding literature. She writes, "Whatever is felt upon the page without being specifically named there—that, one might say, is created. It is the inexplicable presence of the thing not named, of the overtone divined by the ear but not heard by it, the verbal mood, the emotional aura of the fact or the thing or the deed, that gives high quality to the novel or the drama, as well as to poetry itself" ("Willa Cather on Writing" 42-43).

Cather was aware that something took place in literature but that it was something that has no name and likewise *needs* no name. One might place this occurrence within a mystical realm of literature that has the ability to reverberate and bounce off of the imagination of the reader through poetic imagery, and by doing so, create a window into our own unlimited potentiality. In light of Sheldrake's conception of a form of mysticism within Christianity, we would do well to consider how "Whatever we mean by the mystical dimension of Christian faith and practice, I suggest that it both subverts our temptation to settlement and impels us into a condition of perpetual departure" (119). Literature, and specifically as the works of Willa Cather demonstrate, create a

[23] Cather was aware of the great chasm within each individual containing his or her own experiences of time and place. "But the fact remains that one mind finds its richest and deepest material in a time and place that might be anathema to another and that no writer can ever tell in advance what sort of experience is going to be most valuable for him" (Bohlke 133).

space within the place of the imagination which impels us "[...] into a condition of perpetual departure," one that is filled with a potentiality caused by her creation and use of the poetic space found within the self.

References

01. Agamben, Giorgio, *Potentialities: Collected Essays in Philosophy*, Stanford, CA: Stanford University Press, 1999.
02. Bachelard, Gaston, *The Poetics of Space*, trans. Maria Jolas, Boston: Beacon Press, 1958.
03. Bartoloni, Paolo, *Interstitial Writing: Calvino, Caproni, Sereni and Svevo*, Leics, UK: Troubador Publishing Ltd, 2003.
04. Bohlke, L. Brent, Ed. *Willa Cather in Person: Interviews, Speeches, and Letters*. Lincoln: University of Nebraska Press, 1986.
05. Butler, Judith, *Bodies that Matter: On the Discursive Limits of "Sex,"* London: Routledge, 1993.
06. Casey, Edward S., *The Fate of Place: A Philosophical History*, Berkley: University of California Press, 1998.
07. Cather, Willa, *A Lost Lady*, London: Virago. 1923.
08. Cather, Willa, *Alexander's Bridge*, New York: Dover Publications, Inc. 2002.
09. Cather, Willa, *April Twilights*, Gloucestershire, UK: Dodo Press, 2008.
10. Cather, Willa, *Death Comes for the Archbishop*, New York: Vintage Books, 1990.
11. Cather, Willa, *My Antonia* in *Willa Cather: Three Novels*, New York: Carroll & Graf Publishers, Inc. 1988.
12. Cather, Willa, *O Pioneers!* in *Willa Cather: Three Novels*, New York: Carroll & Graf Publishers, Inc. 1988.
13. Cather Willa, *One of Ours*, Lincoln: University of Nebraska Press, 2006.
14. Cather, Willa, *Sapphira and the Slave Girl*, New York: Alfred A. Knopf, 1940.
15. Cather, Willa, *Shadows on the Rock*, Lincoln: University of Nebraska Press, 2006
16. Cather, Willa, *The Professor's House*, Lincoln: University of Nebraska Press, 2002.
17. Certeau, Michel de, *The Practice of Everyday Life*, trans. Steven Rendall, Berkeley: University of California Press, 1984.
18. Davis, Carmel Bendon, *Mysticism and Space: Space and Spatiality in the Works of Richard Rolle, The Cloud of Unknowing Author, and Julian of Norwich*, Washington, DC: The Catholic University of America Press, 2008.

19. Dickinson, Colby, *Agamben and Theology*, London: T&T Clark, 2011.
20. Fryer, Judith, *Felicitous Space: The Imaginative Structures of Edith Wharton and Willa Cather*, Chapel Hill: The University of North Carolina Press, 1986.
21. Gilbert, Sandra M. and Gubar, Susan, *No Man's Land: The Place of the Woman Writer in the Twentieth* Century, Vol. 2, New Haven, CT: Yale University Press, 1991.
22. Hoover, Sharon, ed. *Willa Cather Remembered*, Lincoln: University of Nebraska Press, 2002.
23. Irigaray, Luce, *An Ethics of Sexual Difference*, trans. Carolyn Burke and Gillian C. Gill. New York: Cornell University Press. 1993.
24. Lefebvre, Henri, *The Production of Space*, trans. Donald Nicholson-Smith. Oxford: Blackwell Publishing, 1974.
25. Leonard, Philip. "Ethical Alterities?" in *Self/Same/Other: Re-visioning the Subject in Literature and Theology*, eds. Heather Walton and Andrew W. Hass, Sheffield, England: Sheffield Academic Press, 2000.
26. Quance, Roberta, "Self and Mystical Rebirth in H.D.'s *Trilogy*" in *Self/Same/Other: Re-visioning the Subject in Literature and Theology*, eds. Heather Walton & Andrew W. Hass. Sheffield, England: Sheffield Academic Press, 2000.
27. Rosowski, Susan J., *The Voyage Perilous Willa Cather's Romanticism*, Lincoln, NE: University of Nebraska Press, 1986.
28. Schama, Simon, *Landscape and Memory*, London: HarperCollins, 1995.
29. Sheldrake, Philip, *Spaces for the Sacred*, London: SCM Press, 2001.
30. Slote, Bernice, ed. *The Kingdom of Art: Willa Cather's First Principles and Critical Statements 1893-1896*, Lincoln: University of Nebraska Press, 1966.
31. Watkin, William, *The Literary Agamben: Adventure in Logopoiesis*, New York: Continuum, 2010.

7

"The Moon won't use the Door/Only the Window"
Mystical Romance and the Construction of Voice in the Poems of Jelaludeen Rumi

Dr. Jayanthi Kalpally Puthiyaveetil
Wipro Technologies Ltd, India

> Look inside and find where a person loves from.
> That is the reality, not what they say.
> Hypocrites!
> Give attention to form, the right and wrong way of professing belief.
> Grow instead in universal light.
> When that revealed itself, God gave it a thousand different names,
> the least of those sweet–breathing names being,
> the one who is not in need of anyone.[1]

Jelaludeen Rumi, the Sufi mystic and the founder of the Sufi sect of "whirling dervishes"[2] as they are commonly known, is a poet whose

---

[1] *"Where you love from," Rumi: the Book of Love, 7.* The collection will be referred to henceforth in the paper as RBL: Coleman Barks, *Rumi - The Book of Love: Poems of Ecstasy and Longing*, New York: Harper Collins Publishers, 2003.

[2] A Dervish or Darvesh (from Persian *Darvīsh* via Turkish) is someone treading a Sufi Muslim ascetic path or "Tariqah", known for their extreme poverty and austerity, similar to mendicant friars in Christianity or Hindu/Buddhist/Jain sadhus.(Wikipedia, retrieved, 30Dec2010 from http://en.wikipedia.org/wiki/Dervish)

works have been translated into many tongues across the world and have inspired and continue to inspire the people in their quest for / connect with the Divine. Religious traditions around the world have had differing views on Mysticism. Sufi cult in Islam to which Mewlana Jelaluddin Rumi belongs, focuses the concept of union with God by tapping in the innate knowledge within the individual -as the poem cited above indicates. 'Dervish' or the Sufi mystic focuses on the reparation of the heart and turning it away from all else but God.

Mysticism is a term which has often been (mis-) interpreted in English. The oxford dictionary in 1911 defined mystic as "one who believes in spiritual apprehension of truths beyond the understanding", in a semi contemptuous manner. According to Caroline Spurgeon, the word "has been irresponsibly used over the ages to indicate" any kind of occultism or spiritualism, or any specially curious or fantastic views about God and the universe.[3] The term which has had its origins in the Greco-Roman mystery cults was originally intended to denote the pursuit of a communion with the ultimate reality, super consciousness or God through direct experience or insight. Over the decades, the word has come to connote various things to various religious sects. To Sufis like Rumi, it connotes a connection with the divine even in common every day experiences of the self which are often overlooked by people.

Coleman Barks in his *Introduction: The Magnificent Regions of the Heart* explains the Sufi experience:

> Through Rumi comes a transmission of the divine to this planet in the regions of love. His poetry is a record of his enduring experience of living at the core. In each human being there is a meeting with the divine. That intersection is the heart. (xxi)

The transmission of the divine to Rumi's life and the evolution of his mystic consciousness as manifested his poetry was augmented by his encounter with Shamsi Tabriz, his mentor and friend. This paper will trace the genealogy of Rumi's romance with the Divine, his encounter with his mentor Shams of Tabriz and the construction of the mystical voice in Rumi's poems. In doing so, the paper will also map the parallels

[3] Caroline Spurgeon, *Mysticism in English Literature*, 3.

between the Sufi mystical experience as it evolves through Rumi and various other mystic traditions, particularly those which originated in Asia.

Sufi mystics speak from the region of the heart they call the "qalb" and the experiences cannot fully be defined by words. This awareness was behind my limiting the selection of Rumi poems to one particular collection by Coleman Barks, *Rumi- The Book of Love- Poems of Ecstasy and Longing*. There are several English translations of Rumi's work available for study, like those by Kabir Helminski, Sahram Shiva and Deepak Chopra- to name a few. The selection of the translation here was also rather subjective because the felicity of expressions and language of the heart in Barks's work was something that I could personally connect with. This paper will probably be not very objective or empirical but rather subjective and intuitive in its outlook and exposition since I want to be as true as possible to the experience of Rumi and the feeling/experience his poetry would evoke in the regions of the listener's heart.

Robert Graves in his *Introduction to* Idries Shah's work *The Sufis* explains the mystical evolution that Sufis undergo:

> The individual devotee is offered a 'secret garden' for his understanding, but never required to become a monk, nun or hermit, like the more conventional mystics; and he thereafter claims to be enlightened by actual experience- 'he who tastes knows, not by philosophic argument'. (viii)

Sufi mystical culture is similar to Zen Buddhism in its emphasis on living in the present moment, in the power of silence and its understanding of the Divine essence through experiences, often considered ordinary or mundane. Sufi practice is very different from the Jnana marga or Advaitha of the Hindus which gives a lot of importance to rational thought and philosophic argument along with the spiritual experience and devotion in its understanding of the Divine. "It is different from the Christian mystical thought [...] whereas Christian mystics regard ecstasy as a union with God, and therefore the height of their religious attainment, Sufis admit its value only if the devotee can afterwards return to the world and live in a manner consonant with his experience" (*Graves*, xvi).

Graves also attributes the beginning of Freemasonry to the Sufi mystics and traces the genesis of the three working instruments on modern Masonic lodges to the three postures of prayer, a result of the influence of the Arab cultures on the early Knight Templars. However, this connection cannot be fully examined since the Masonic mystical practices are often very closely guarded and hence remain inaccessible to outsiders. Sufi, mystics, however differ from Freemasons in that "they transcend outer religious forms" and sees outer religion only as "a prelude to special experience" (*Shah*, 29).

Sufi experience cannot be apprehended or summarized only through the world of the intellect. In the words of Idries Shah: "If it is felt that the truth about extra physical fact must be sought only through a certain way of thinking, the rational and "scientific" one, there can be no contact between the Sufi and the supposedly objective seeker" (xxiv). The external world –the empirical one is definitely there, the world of forms, but the seeker should not just see this- s/he needs to also see the world of the spirit that is manifested through this world of forms and the oneness in these. In Rumi's words:

> The disc of the sun does exist, but if you see
> only the ray bodies, you may have doubts
> The human divine combinations are a oneness.
> Plurality the apparent separation into rays [...]
>
> (*The Granary*, 177)

Sufis don't discredit the experiences of this world or of the senses. They see the world of the spirit and experiences of this world as "wings of the same bird". In this sense, a Sufi way is very similar to the Tantric or Vama Margi/Aghori path the aim of which- Robert Svabodha in his book *Aghora: At the left of God* explains as, "Laya, return of the seeker to the state of undifferentiated existence" (21). Sufis like Rumi, unlike the Tantrics, do not subscribe to elaborate ritualistic practices in order to achieve this "laya." They, however, use images of human love or the act of sex to cement its perspicuous perception of the Divine. The poem *Sexual urgency and True Virility,* in its narration of the love of the Captain of the Caliph of Egypt for the beautiful concubine of the King of Mosul highlights this:

> When the Captain sees her,
> he falls in love like the Caliph.
> Don't laugh at this.
> Their loving is also part of infinite love, without which
> the world does not evolve.
>
> Objects move from inorganic
> to vegetation, to selves endowed with spirit,
> through the urgency of every love
> that wants to consummate [...].

Rumi's poem abound in such images of love and every day experience- the man and the maid who consummate their love outwitting the jealous wife, dough being moulded into bread, the tailor who cuts the cloth in order to sew them, ants moving grains of wheat etc. The lines cited below from the Rumi poem *The Public Bath* beautifully connects the wórld of the spirit with the world of experience/senses through its symbolism of the "phenomenal world as a furnace for heating water for the public bath":

> The mystery is how the obsessions of the
> of the furnace stokers keep the bathwaters
> of the others simmering perfectly.
>
> They seem opposed, but they're necessary
> to each other's work: the proud piling up of
> fire worship, the humble disrobing
> and emptying out of purification.
>
> As the sun dries wet dung to make it
> ready to heat water, so dazzling
> spark fly from the burning filth. (74)

Rumi's poems through the sensory experiences of the lover take us to the realm of mystic love. Barks elucidate this thus: "Love is the connection with spirit, and one way it flows through is form. That is the state of rapture Rumi praises, the joy of being inside an intersection with the divine which is what this world is" (18).This intersection is the source of the music in his soul, his muse and the poems which emerge mellifluously. It is also Rumi's meeting place with Shams of Tabriz, his friend and mentor:

In your light I learn how to love.
In your beauty, how to make poems.
You dance inside my chest
where no one sees you, but sometimes I do,
and that sight becomes this art. (7)

Rumi poem *Put this design in your carpet* hails "spiritual experience" "as a modest woman how looks lovingly at one man" (20). In reading Rumi, one feels tempted to echo the words of Oscar Wilde: "There is nothing that cures the senses but the soul, and nothing that will cure the soul but the senses" (Cf. Wilber, 1998, vii)

Rumi poems also talks about the need to live and act in the present-ness of the present: "The source of now is here" (*This is enough*, 22*)*. Sufi mystical thought in this respect is a bit similar to Zen Buddhism. In fact, all religions/spiritual practices across the world, talk of the power of the present moment to transcend its present-ness, while retaining its essence. Rumi poem entitled by Barks as, *Begin* talks about need for acting/acquiring spiritual awareness in the present without postponing it or clouding it with the burden of thought:

This is now. Now is. Don't postpone till then.
Spend the spark of iron on stone.
Sit at the head of the table.
Dip your spoon in the bowl.
Seat yourself next to your joy
and have your awakened soul pour wine.
Branches in the spring wind,
easy dance of jasmine and cypress.

Cloth for green robes has been cut from pure absence.
You are the tailor, settled among his shop goods, quietly sewing. (24)

The awareness of the present through the experience of the senses tempers Rumi's understanding of Divine love: "Loving God is the only pleasure/Other delights hurt the soul" (*What Hurts the Soul*, 88).

Rumi's mystic romance with the Divine is also manifested in his relationship with his friend and mentor Shamsi Tabriz. There are numerous legends/versions surrounding Rumi's encounter with Shamsi Tabriz on November 15, 1244 – a mystical occurrence that changed Rumi's life.[4] Shamsi Tabriz was longing for a friend and companion to accompany him on his spiritual journey. Apparently, a mystical voice guided him to Konya where he met Rumi. There are different versions about Rumi's first meeting with Shams. In one version, Rumi was reading a book with a large stack of books in front of him. On seeing this, Shams is believed to have asked Rumi what he was reading. Rumi took a look at the disheveled stranger clad in black and seems to have replied scathingly: "Something you don't understand". On hearing this, Shams threw the books into the stream nearby .Rumi hastily rescued the books and to his surprise, he found them to be completely dry. On seeing this, Rumi seems to have asked Shams what it was to which Shams gave the same reply "Something you don't understand". This legend or the various versions of this legend apart from celebrating the onset of mystic transformation in Rumi also symbolically highlights the Sufi belief that mystical experiences cannot be learned in a didactic manner. The poem *The Basket of Fresh Bread* elucidates this:

If you want dervish hood, spiritual poverty
and emptiness, you must be friends with a teacher.
Talking about it, reading books, and doing practices don't help.
Soul receives from soul that knowing. (65)

[4] Shams had traveled throughout the Middle East searching and praying for someone who could "endure my company." A voice said to him, "What will you give in return?" Shams replied, "My head!" The voice then said, "The one you seek is Jalal ud-Din of Konya" (Wikipedia, retrieved 01Jan2010 from http://en.wikipedia.org/wiki/Rumi).

Various Hindu and Buddhist cults also celebrate the role of Guru or teacher in initiating a seeker into the ways of the Divine. The dohas of Kabir Das in the Bhakthi movement particularly the one entitled "Guru Mahima" celebrates the role of the guru: "guru govind dono khade, kis ko lage panw; balihari guru apko, govind diyo lakhai" (If the guru and Govind (Lord Krishna) are standing together, at whose feet will you bow down first? I am a sacrifice onto the guru for he has revealed Govind to me).[5] We also find the celebration of the role of Guru or the teacher in the *Guru Ashtakam* of Sri Sankaracharya.[6]

Rumi poem *Zikr* highlights the role of the teacher in getting the seeker out of the complacence of every day comforts:

> Light is the image of your teacher.
> Your enemies love the dark.
> A spider weaves a web over a light,
> out of herself makes a veil.
>
> Pray for a tough instructor to hear
> and act and stay within you.
> We have been busy accumulating solace
> Make us afraid of how we were. (95-96)

This is what exactly Shams seems to have done to Rumi. The poem also subtly plays on the name Shams, which literally means "the sun" or the source of light.

Shamsi Tabriz was the sun who melted the darkness of ego / complacence in Rumi's soul/life and filled it with the light of wisdom. The poem *The Wrist* in Barks' collection highlights how Rumi was able to - like the spider- "draw the web over the light":

---

[5] The translation of Kabir Doha "Guru Mahima" is taken from *The Greatness of the Guru* by Dr. J. Das for Sadguru Prakatya Dham, Kabirbagh, Varanasi, retrieved, 2 Jan 2011, from http://www.hajursaheb.com/html/guru_mahima.html.

[6] The translation of *Guru Ashtakam* by Swami Vivekananda is available on You Tube: http://www.youtube.com/watch?v=QqCji-oDTlA.

Who are you? The inner vision of consciousness?
The heart? A sacred half-light, are you that?
Do you grow gatherings? Are you a friend
of the sun who comes and goes so quickly?
Do not forget your vertical passage, the night of power,
and don't hide from the one
for whom all our secrets are down in the pillow under
his head, doctor of lovers, soul for this thick world,
the one who spirals iron
like dough and makes the body lightedness.
No belief is necessary to enter this tent
where one love story changes to another.
I remember that with these words brought here
by a falcon from the wrist of Shams. (111)

As the sun disappears in the evening sky after filling the day with light, Shams too disappeared[7] unannounced from Rumi's life one fine day- this external removal only served to heighten his inner connectedness to the Divine. Even though Rumi mourned his physical separation from Shams for a while- his collection of poems *Divani Shamsi Tabriz* bears testimony to this he was soon able to understand that this physical removal was necessary to attain an inner connectedness - for the transformation of "one love story" into another and to transcend the binaries of existence and essence/lover and beloved: "If the beloved is everywhere, /the lover is a veil /but when Living itself/becomes the friend/lovers disappear." (112)

All the mystic, tantric or yogic traditions in Asia celebrate the role of the teacher/ mentor/ master/ guru in initiating an aspirant to a particular path. Rumi's mystic love for Shams is similar to Radha's love for Krishna or Vivekananda's love for his teacher Sri. Ramakrishna Paramahamsa - symbolic of the love of the individual soul for the eternal

[7] There are various versions about Shams sudden disappearance from Rumi's life. Shams suddenly disappeared unannounced from Rumi's life after kindling the mystic fire in Rumi and transforming him. Shams stayed with Rumi for two years and they even spend forty days together in isolation. One version says that Shams was murdered by the jealous disciples of Rumi. This version however, is not substantiated by many scholars and critics.

or Divine which it glimpses through the medium of guru or the teacher. The poem *The Company of Lovers* highlights the transformative power of this love:

> If you want to know God, enjoy the company of lovers.
> If you want to be thought a great person,
> learn the subtle point and say it with many variations
> as the answer to every question.
> If you want to live your soul,
> find a friend like Shams and stay near. (142)

Under the influence of Shamsi Tabriz, Rumi's mystic consciousness underwent a transformation and he was able to transcend "the nonsense categories of *there* and *here*, /race, nation, religion, /starting point and destination" (13) and experience the power of Divine love and the purpose of human existence as the poem *Response to your Question* elucidates:

> You are soul, and you *are* love
> not a sprite or an angel or a human being!
> You're a *Godman-womanGod-manGod-Godwoman!*
> No more questions now
> As to what its we're *doing* here. (14)

The realization of the presence of the divinity or Godhead in the human soul is what most mystical traditions aim at. Self realization is what all religions espouse. In Rumi's case, this was possible only through the help and instruction of his teacher and friend, Shams. Rumi attributes his mystic vision of world to Shams who taught him the art of "seeing," as evidenced in the poem *Special Plates*:

> Notice how each particle moves.
> Notice how everyone has just arrived here from a journey.
> Notice how each wants a different food.
> Notice how the stars vanish as the sun comes up,
> and how all the streams stream towards the ocean.

Look at the chefs preparing special plates
for everyone according to what they need.
Look at this cup that can hold the ocean.
Look at those who see the face.
Look through Shams' eyes into water that is entirely jewels.
(13-14)

The transformation, from an ordinary erudite scholar who studied religion, to a mystic who understood the power of love with the help of Shams, who walked with him in silence, lends a different hue to Rumi's poetry, which as Barks points out flows from the region of heart which he calls "qalb". For the volume of mystic poetry that had sprung from his intuitive heart to emerge as they are now, Rumi first had to understand the power of seeing in the silence beyond the language- door:

At night, I open the window and ask
the moon to come and press its face against mine.
Breathe into me.
Close the language -door and open the love- window
The moon won't use the door
Only the window. (*Some Kiss We Want*, 34)

It is this awaressness that Divinity reveals itself only when you open your heart window that has given Rumi's poetry its peculiar form. In one sense, it is poetry of the highest order-in the sense that it produces what Idries Shah terms as a "strangely complex exultation" (132) in the consciousness of the reader or the listener. Yet in other ways, it breaks all the rules of conventional verse/prose in its rather intricate presentation of ideas/experiences.

Rumi's writing is very modern its form and presentation but not modernistic or intellectual in the way the poetry of the modern poets T.S Eliot or Ezra Pound is. There is a felicity of expression that comes unbounded from his deepest self that makes his writing magical/ mystical:

> Nothing can stay bound or be imprisoned.
> You say, "End this poem here and
> Wait for what's next." I will.
> Poems are rough notations for the music we are. (*The Music We are*, 27)

Rumi's poems contain fables, jokes, anecdotes, references to popular tales, religious texts like Koran, Torah, and the Bible, conversations with Shams and his other teachers.[8] Idries Shah calls this "the method of scatter, whereby a picture is built up by multiple impacts to infuse into the mind the Sufi message." (133)

Mikhail Bakhtin's concept of "polyphony" can be suitably deployed to map the construction of the mystic voice in Rumi's poems. Rumi's narratives are dialogic in nature. Mikhail Bakhtin in *Problems of Dostoevsky's Poetics* (1976) explains the dialogic position:

> It should be pointed out that the inevitability of a single and unified consciousness by no means necessarily follows from the concept of the one and only truth (*edinaia istina*) itself. It is completely possible to imagine that this one and only truth requires a plurality of consciousnesses and it has so to speak, the nature of an event and is born in the point of contact of various consciousnesses (65).

This is what one can perceive in the narrative voice of Jalaludeen Rumi. One can find different voices colliding within the mystic voice of Rumi- the scriptures, popular tales, discourses and conversations with Shams- to name a few. Each of these have an independent existence even as they collide/ cohere/ collude to create the poetic voice of Rumi- thus creating what Bakhtin terms as "polyphony": "the principles of several converging stories which in contrasting ways augment each

---

[8] The poems "Imaru'l-Quays", "Zuleikha", "Uzayr", " Nasuhs' Changing", "The Death of Saladin," "The Prince of Kabul," etc in Barks collection uses the fables to convey various spiritual themes. Many of the poems abound in references to Jesus, Prophet Muhammed, Moses and the religious texts. In fact, all these contribute to create the amalgam that is Rumi's mystic voice.

other and are connected in accordance with the musical principle of polyphony" (35).

What makes Rumi's narratives unique is the fact that there is no conscious craftsmanship anywhere and the polyphony is generated naturally as the Rumi poem *Who Says Words with My Mouth* elucidates:

> This poetry. I never know what I'm going to say.
> I don't plan it.
> When I am outside the saying of it,
> I get very quiet and rarely speak at all. (57)

The construction of the mystical voice in the poems is thus not an act of conscious will, but "a way of love" that defies any "subtle argument"(49).The experience of the mystic consciousness shapes the patterns that emerge in the poems and one definitely can echo here with Rumi:

> No better love than love with no object,
> no more satisfying work than work with no purpose.
> If you could give up tricks and cleverness
> that would be the cleverest trick (147)

Even as I look for patterns while writing this paper, I realize that Rumi's narratives break all patterns, and that I too should give "up tricks and cleverness" if I have to connect with the deep mystery and the beauty of silence, Rumi's poems talk about. I too, want to experience Rumi's poems in the recesses of my heart, like Shiva's cosmic dance and the sound of his dhamru, as I long for my tryst with the eternal, and follow the Masters who say "Chidanandarumpam [...] Shivoham Shivoham!"[9] as the cosmic play of the Shakthi moves and turns the consciousness inward.

[9] *Niravana Ashtakam* or *Atma Shatakam* by Sri Sankaracharya. is available on you tube:
http://www.youtube.com/watch?v=_AHBSi2_Dpc&feature=related.

References

01. Bakhtin, M.M., *Problems of Dostoevsky's Poetics*, trans. R.W. Rostel, USA: Ardis, 1976

02. Barks, Coleman, *Rumi: The Book of Love: Poems of Ecstasy and Longing*, New York: Harper Collins Publishers, 2003.

03. Das, J., "Guru Mahima," *The Greatness of Guru*, Varanasi: Sad guru Prakatya Dham. Retrieved,2Jan2011, from, "Dervish, " *Wikipedia*, retrieved, 30Dec2010 ,from
http://www.hajursaheb.com/html/guru_mahima.html

04. "Dervish, " *Wikipedia*, retrieved, 30Dec2010 ,from http://en.wikipedia.org/wiki/Dervish

05. Freke, Timothy, ed. *Lao Tzu's Tao Te Ching*, London: Paitkus, 1995.

06. Graves, Robert, "Introduction," in Idries Shah, *The Sufis*, New York: Anchor Books, 1971.

07. Lin, Derek, *Tao Te Ching: Annotated and Explained*, New Delhi: Rupa &Co, 2010.

08. One Hand Clapping: A Collection of Zen Stories, New Delhi: Rupa & Co, 2003.

09. "Rumi," *Wikipedia*, retrieved, 01Jan 2010, from, http://en.wikipedia.org/wiki/Rumi

10. Spurgeon, Caroline, *Mysticism in English Literature*. E-book no.11935.USA: Public Domain: Released on 1st April 2004, retrieved, 2nd Jan2010 from http://www.gutenberg.org/files/11935/11935-h/11935-h.htm

11. Sri Adi Shankaracharya. "Guru Ashtakam". *You Tube*, trans, Swami Vivekananda, retrieved 30th Dec2010,from http://www.youtube.com/watch?v=QqCji-oDTlA

12. Sri Adi Shankaracharya. "Atma Shatakam or Nirvanana Ashtakam," *You tube*, trans. Swami Vivekananda, retrieved 29thDec2011, from, http://www.youtube.com/ watch?v=_AHBSi2_Dpc&feature=related

13. Svabodha, Robert. E., *Aghora: At the Left Hand of God*, New Delhi: Rupa & Co, 1986.

14. Wilber, Ken, *The Marriage of Sense and Soul: Integrating Science and Religion*, Boston: Gateway-Shambala Publications, 1998.

8

Music and Mysticism

The Emergence of Musical Meaning

Dr. Marlies de Munck
Institute of Philosophy, K.L. Leuven, Belgium

All over the world, in virtually all cultures that we know of, music's peculiar power to alter people's awareness and to induce experiences of a loss of the self has secured it a prominent place in rituals and ceremonies of all sorts. Thanks to its easy access to the emotions music is not only a remarkably efficacious means to open up our hearts, it also functions, and has done so in all times, as an invitation to explore the vast fields of experience beyond the well-ordered domain of rationality and the familiarity of self-consciousness. According to the French musicologist Jules Combarieu music originated in magical practices and was primarily used to charm the gods and so wield power over this world.[1]

Through the singing of incantations—literally en*chant*ments—man sought to make contact with an otherworldly realm in order to influence daily life by temporarily transgressing it. Thus, music was originally used as a tool by shamans, magicians, sorcerers, witches and medicine men to get into an ecstatic state of trance or it served as part of meditation rituals and techniques—repetitive drumbeats, for instance, or singing and humming seem to be highly effective in this regard—

[1] Jules Combarieu, *La musique et la magie. Etude sur les origines populaires de l'art musical, son influence et sa fonction dans les sociétés*, Paris: Alphonse Picard et fils, 1909, 9.

eventually to affect the world and bring about change. The effectiveness of music's magic thus relied on its capacity to make contact with another, transcendent world.

However, since the beginning of western philosophical thought, music's original bond with magic and mysticism has been systematically underplayed and even deliberately repressed by relegating music to the role of obedient servant of the word. In the *Republic*, for instance, Socrates pays careful attention to the kinds and modes of music that are to be included in the education of the guardians of the ideal state. At once he reminds Glaucon that the playing of purely instrumental music with all its extravaganzas and embellishments should be forbidden, "for our principle is that rhythm and harmony are regulated by the words, and not the words by them."[2] No doubt, the ghastly spectacle of delirious *bacchantes* must have hovered before Plato's mental eye while writing this whole passage on the role of music in the state. Indeed, in *The Birth of Tragedy* Nietzsche describes vividly how, according to him, the power of music was used by the followers of Dionysus to violently overrule the *principium individuationis*. In the frenzy of dancing to the sounds of the *aulos,* "these Dionysian emotions awake, which, as they intensify, cause the subjective to vanish into complete self-forgetfulness."[3] However, music was not exclusively tied to occult practices. In ancient Greece the cult of Dionysus knew its perfect counterweight in the worship of Apollo, who played the *lyre*, a stringed instrument that, with its soft and gentle sounds, was perfectly suited to accompany the reciting of poetry. Obviously, in the service of words the music was at once tied down to clearly intuitable contents, which made it considerably less suspicious from a rational point of view. This kind of censure on certain types of music—or on art in general—in order to restrict their influence on our mood and behavior is a clear instance of what the American philosopher Arthur Danto, more than two-thousand years later, famously called the 'philosophical disenfranchisement of art': "the first philosophical responses to art were in effect theories, the political purpose of which

---

[2] Plato, *Republic*, trans. Benjamin Jowett, New York: Barnes & Noble Books, 2004, 94.

[3] Friedrich Nietzsche, *The Birth of Tragedy*, trans. Clifton P. Fadiman, New York: Dover Publications, 1995, 3.

was to extrude art, somehow, from the possibility of efficacy, and lodge it, metaphysically or institutionally, where it could do us no harm."[4] Only after having been 'domesticated' could music start to aspire to a place among the other fine arts. First and foremost, however, it has been as an accompaniment to Christian liturgy that music was allowed to play a role in western 'high' culture.

Paradoxically, the gradual emancipation of western classical music from its subsidiary relation to the word—culminating in the early 19th century with the rise and glory of absolute music—did not dislodge the deeply ingrained prejudices that had always been held against it. On the contrary, this very evolution has, at least on a theoretical level, confirmed the age-old philosophical aversion to music's intoxicating potential. Paradigmatic in this regard are the writings of Eduard Hanslick, a famous 19th century music critic. In his highly influential essay *Vom Musikalisch Schönen* he launched a thesis that for more than a century remained the credo of academic music theorists, claiming that music is nothing but 'tonally moving forms'.[5] With this strange little formula Hanslick meant to say nothing more or less than that music's means and ends fully coincide. Or, in other words, musical forms do not contain, signify or refer to extra-musical 'contents'. If music has a meaning at all, Hanslick stated, it cannot be anything but the music itself—its bare sounding structures in time. Admittedly, the author was reacting against a veritable abundance of romantic, exalted superlatives that were current in his day. Under the influence of the romantic *Kunstreligion* music came to be considered the highest of all arts, precisely because it was held to be able—thanks to its lack of immediate, representational content—to guide the audience to higher, transcendent atmospheres.[6] The danger of

[4] Arthur Danto, *Beyond the Brillo Box*, Berkeley: University of California Press, 1992, 184. Danto first introduced this hypothesis in his essay 'The Philosophical Disenfranchisement of Art,' *Grand Street*, Vol. 4, No. 3 (Spring, 1985), 171-189.

[5] Eduard Hanslick, *On the Musically Beautiful: A Contribution Towards the Revision of the Aesthetics of Music*, trans. Geoffrey Payzant, Indianapolis: Hackett, 1986, 29.

[6] See, for instance, E.T.A Hoffmann's famous reviews in the *Allgemeine Musikalische Zeitung* of compositions by Beethoven—notably the fifth symphony—or his many texts featuring the imaginary character of 'Kapellmeister Johannes Kreisler', in which music was elevated to the status of the highest, most romantic and powerful of all the arts. Cf. David Charlton, ed. *E.T.A. Hoffmann's Musical Writings: Kreisleriana; The*

such absolute veneration of music, as Hanslick saw it, is that in the end the music itself risks being overlooked in favor of whatever lies behind or beyond its tones. It could become a means in order to trigger emotional or semi-religious experiences, or an enigmatic code to be cracked as a mere vehicle for a mysterious content. In order to defend music's own rights, therefore, Hanslick not only rejected the idea of a musical 'meaning' besides the *tönend bewegte Formen*, he also strenuously objected to any view that unscientifically turned music into a stimulant for emotional, religious or ecstatic experiences. "Incidentally," he wrote, "for people who want the kind of effortless suppression of awareness they get from music, there is a wonderful recent discovery which far surpasses that art. We refer to ether and chloroform."[7]

Ever since, at least in the tradition of the western fine arts, we have learned to be more disciplined and to appreciate music as an end in itself. At the same time, however, all this well-deserved respect for its artistic autonomy appears to have obfuscated our understanding of how music can be experienced as deeply and emotionally meaningful. It is not so easy to see how musical structures, being nothing more, after all, than a series of combined frequencies in time—a purely quantitative phenomenon—are able to engender such enthusiasm among listeners as they apparently do. Harder still, is it to understand how listening to a series of frequencies can be experienced as a deeply touching and emotional affair, far transcending the mathematical and intellectual pleasures of recognizing harmony and regularity of form. Still, Hanslick was certainly right when he pointed out that instrumental music does not rely on referential relations the way language does: even though its structures may remind of the structures of linguistic grammar, it does not consist of the fixed, separate elements of a proper vocabulary. Although it is certainly an expressive medium, music cannot be simply analyzed as yet another sign-system since it does not point to a well-circumscribable or paraphrasable meaning outside itself that it would be expressive of.[8] On the other hand, the way in which we experience a

Poet and the Composer; Music Criticism, trans. M. Clarke, Cambridge: Cambridge University Press, 2003.

[7] Eduard Hanslick, *On the Musically Beautiful*, 59.

[8] For the sake of the argument I restrict my analysis here to the case of purely instrumental, so-called 'absolute' music, as this poses the highest number of philosophical questions

piece of music is not completely arbitrary either—not *anything* goes—and this, of course, is puzzling.

In *The Critique of Judgement* Immanuel Kant made an apt observation pertaining to another great puzzle in aesthetics, namely the judgment of the beautiful. He pointed out that whenever we differ in opinion about the artistic merits of a particular work of art, we do feel entitled to quarrel over it because certain interpretations just seem to fit the work better than others. That is, according to Kant, there is a sense in which we could say that a work's beauty is 'objective': "If he [i.e. the spectator] gives out anything as beautiful, he supposes in others the same satisfaction; he judges not merely for himself, but for everyone, and speaks of beauty as if it were a property of things. Hence he says 'the *thing* is beautiful'; and he does not count on the agreement of others with this his judgment of satisfaction, because he has found this agreement several times before, but he *demands* it of them. He blames them if they judge otherwise and he denies them taste, which he nevertheless requires from them."[9] Now, could we not say something similar about musical meaning? Doesn't the meaningfulness of music appear to us as something that surpasses the level of strictly personal, arbitrary experience? Hence, are we not allowed to say that this meaning is part of the order of, if not human-independent 'objectivity', then at least 'intersubjectivity'?

During the second half of the 20th century many theorists have tried to accommodate a growing need to reconnect music with the emotions and even with extra-musical contents in order to philosophically understand and ground the experience of musical meaning. Yet, as it turned out, it was rather difficult to bridge the theoretical gap that by then had opened up between music and the emotions, without doing injustice either to the music itself or to its evident meaningfulness. It is not entirely surprising, therefore, that the philosophy of music soon became a booming business in which one of the key-questions was precisely this: what is the meaning of a piece of (western, classical, absolute) music? This issue often

---

with regard to musical meaning. Obviously, the case of program music considerably differs in this respect, as do the genres of song and opera.

[9] Immanuel Kant, *Critique of Judgement, trans.* J. H. Bernard, New York: Hafner Press, 1951, 47 (emphasis in original).

turned into a somewhat strange problem, namely: where should we look for the meaning of music? Many hypotheses have come up in light of this basic problem, some of which maintained—referring to Hanslick's formalistic position—that, if there is something like an 'objective' musical meaning, it can only reside within the structures of the music itself, while others have suggested that it is all a matter of recovering the composer's or the performer's intentions. Still others have defended that musical meaning can only exist in the listener's mind, aroused by the music as a physical or psychological effect of it. Most theorists have tried to develop a more nuanced middle position, though, for instance by further elaborating on Hanslick's formalism while subtly letting the listener's emotions reenter the stage.[10] However, the use of such terms as 'pure form' and 'content'—or the very concept of 'meaning' itself, for that matter—makes it very difficult, if not impossible, to localize the searched-for meaning of music. Moreover, many have argued that, under the dominant influence of formalistic and neo-formalistic theories, a rational understanding of music as a highly complex structure has become disproportionately important so that having a true musical experience now seems to be a matter of expertise, excluding the lay music lover who genuinely believed, up till then, having meaningful musical experiences as well. All in all, one has to admit that the quest for the meaning of music is not only symptomatic of an age in which we seem to have lost our intuitive understanding of these matters, the very quest itself actually appears to make it even harder to explain why music matters to virtually everyone and has done so in all places and all times. Picking up the question about musical meaning myself, I want to argue that a reconsideration of music's original ties with the mystical experience may open a new route and perhaps lead us out of the philosophical impasse.

If we shift our ground to the musical experience we can start the investigation from the plain phenomenological observation that music *is* meaningful for us, not as a content-wrapped-in-a-form, nor as a form-without-a-content, but as something that is revealed in and by the music whenever we actually engage in it. In the musical experience

[10] E.g. Peter Kivy's theory of 'enhanced formalism' in: Peter Kivy, *Introduction to a Philosophy of Music*, Oxford: Clarendon Press, 2002, 88-109.

we are faced with a kind of meaning that is radically different from the referential type of linguistic meaning that is all too easily taken as a paradigm of meaning *tout court*. Indeed, a number of important twentieth century philosophers have pointed out that meaning does not reside either inside or outside things but rather emerges from the relations *between* things. According to Robert Nozick, "[f]or a life to have meaning, it must connect with other things, with some things or values beyond itself. Meaning, and not merely of lives, seems to lie in such connections. To ask something's meaning is to ask how it is connected, perhaps in specified ways, to other things."[11] Indeed, it does not seem implausible to assume, as Aldous Huxley does in *The Doors of Perception*, that the quest for meaning is born out of a need to transcend the limits of self-conscious individuality in order to relate to something other than the self: "Most men and women lead lives at the worst so painful, at the best so monotonous, poor and limited that the urge to escape, the longing to transcend themselves if only for a few moments, is and has always been one of the principal appetites of the soul. Art and religion, carnivals and saturnalia, dancing and listening to oratory – all these have served, in H.G. Well's phrase, as Doors in the Wall."[12] As a consequence, every successful form of self-transcendence may be experienced as meaningful in some way or another. Indeed, according to Nozick, again, "the particular things or causes people find make their life feel meaningful all take them beyond their own narrow limits and connect them up with something else. Children, relationships with other persons, helping others, advancing justice, continuing and transmitting a tradition, pursuing truth, beauty, world betterment—these and the rest link you to something wider than yourself."[13]

In this light it is useful to begin with the question why we are so attracted to music—*why do we care about it at all?* If the typically human quest for meaning is born out of a primary urge to transcend the inherent loneliness of the self, we may be susceptible for the call of anything other-than-the-self that offers us something to relate to. This

[11] Robert Nozick, *Philosophical Explanations*, Cambridge: Harvard University Press, 1981, 594.

[12] Aldous Huxley, *The Doors of Perception and Heaven and Hell*, New York: Harper & Row, 1990, 62.

[13] Robert Nozick, *Philosophical Explanations*, 595.

seems to be the case with music: whenever it appeals to us it calls for our attention and invites us to engage in it. And when we do so, when we manage to actively participate in the music in some way or another, we experience it as being genuinely meaningful. So, by asking why we care about music, the philosophical problem of musical meaning arises within the broader, dynamic context of the active practice of listening to music. Conversely, the 'narrow' question as to *what* the meaning of a work is inevitably objectifies the meaning, 'freezes' and hypostatizes it so that it is easily conceived of as an autonomous content that, as it turns out, is nowhere to be found in the musical forms. As the mysterious counterpart of a *flatus musicalis* it is almost asking to be cut away by the formalist's razor.

If we 'zoom out', however, and reformulate the philosophical question so that it takes into account the factor of lived experience, we can focus on the act of listening, which is where we first become aware of the work as being meaningful. In doing so, we withdraw music's meaning from the metaphysical realm and firmly put it back within the order of daily life. In other words, we should look carefully at what happens when we listen to music in order to understand why we care to listen to it in the first place and, closely connected to that, to see how we come to experience it the way we do. Here, we find that within the act of relating to music by actively participating in its sounds we connect to something 'else': a heterogeneous element that transcends our subjective consciousness. We connect to the music as to an outsider, for instance, when we trace and try to rebuild its structures or when we make imaginative associations, wondering how it will proceed. We also connect to the music, however, when we dance to it, or merely tap a foot on its rhythms—in fact, there are so many different ways to engage in music that we cannot even start to list them here. They all have at least one thing in common, though, which is the fact that the music takes us on a particular journey through time. It appeals to us, invites us, takes us up and carries us away. We may hear the music as expressive of the emotions of the composer or the performer or as mirroring our own feelings and thoughts, we may hear it as a particular embodiment of abstract time or as the musical expression of an extra-musical scene or narrative, etcetera, etcetera. It actually does not really matter for our present purpose *how* exactly we experience the music—that is, *what* the music means to us—what matters here is that all these 'as if's' are ways to give voice to our intuition that it is something else, something coming from outside, that we encounter in the music. Hearing the music as if it were this or that shows that we experience the meaning not as a mere product of our imagination or a projection of our searching, hungry souls.

In my opinion, this is precisely the kind of meaning that makes up the core of every worthwhile musical experience. In order to further explore this crucial aspect of heterogeneity, let us have a look at the case of so-called 'strongly embodied symbols'. As Paul Moyaert points out, there is a 'primitive' way to conceive of symbols so that they are not experienced as conventional signs—say, 'signifiers'—but rather as places where two realities coincide. Opening his chapter on icons, Moyaert quotes Gerardus Van der Leeuw to underpin his view: "For the primitive mentality, though, 'symbol' is precisely what the word means, namely a coincidence of two realities. 'It means' is, primitively speaking, equal to: it is. We say that a statue symbolizes God, but 'of course' is not divine itself. For primitive man the idol is god, not that it is equal in all respects, but the god participates in his image and the image in the god."[14] According to Moyaert, this so-called primitive understanding of symbols is still part, even when mostly implicit, of our symbolic sensitivity today. Our way of dealing with symbols—we are drawn to them physically, want to touch, hold, see, hear them—reveals that we do not experience them to be entirely external to the reality they represent: "By representing reality, the symbol takes in something of the power of that reality's meaning. This transfer of meaning distinguishes symbols from signs. Symbols not only enable us to refer to or to make connections with what is not actually given (for instance ideal reality, the supersensible, the invisible). No, they are an embodiment and an actualization of the reality for which they stand. They are part of what they represent."[15] Thus, symbols strongly embody whatever they represent when we experience their materiality as containing something

[14] Gerardus van der Leeuw, *De primitieve mens en de religie*, Groningen: Batavia, 1937, 41, quoted in: Paul Moyaert, *Iconen en beeldverering*, 141 (my translation).
[15] Paul Moyaert, *Iconen en beeldverering*, 146 (my translation).

of the very being of that referent. In some cases, however, a symbol does no longer signify a meaning external to it at all because the meaning has entirely sunken into the symbol itself, it has sneaked into its concrete materiality. Or, to put it differently, the symbol has pushed the original referent out of the picture and embodies its meaning no longer vicariously but immediately.

Be that as it may, it still may seem a little odd to say that music—especially instrumental music—is a symbol since it does not seem to have any referent to begin with. Still, according to Jules Combarieu, music "has lost its role as an efficient tool to become a pure symbol."[16] This claim becomes very interesting, however, if we regard music as a kind of *strongly embodied* symbol in the latter sense—that is, as a symbol that over time has become pregnant of its own meaning, no longer referring to it as to an external something but incarnating it in and by its particular material manifestation. Could it be, then, that in the act of relating to music we experience the alterity of that other realm—the transcendent order to which music used to relate the shaman and the sorcerer—as materially embodied in and by the autonomous musical tones? As we saw earlier, when listening to music we do in fact participate in a time-space that we have neither arranged by ourselves, nor projected onto the world. Indeed, the otherness of musical time is precisely what allows for a true relation with it and thus, recalling Nozick, for us to experience it as meaningful. On the other hand, whenever we fail to connect to the music, when it does not appeal to us or when we don't know how to relate to it, as is often the case when we encounter music from a strange, remote culture, or experimental music that breaks with all the rules with which we have acquainted ourselves, the meaning escapes us and the music remains mute, even though we can physically hear its tones.

From the point of view of the musical experience, from within the process of trying, succeeding or failing to engage in the music, of feeling the call to surrender or rather being pushed away, we can start to qualitatively understand how diverse the phenomenon of musical meaning can and must be. It is continually in flux, not only because of music's ephemeral character but because musical meaning is an

---

[16] Jules Combarieu, *La musique et la magie*, 6 : "ce qui était d'abord un moyen d'action réputé efficace a pu devenir un pur symbole." (my translation)

emergent quality of a praxis: the active, intentional process of relating to the sounds. In order for any such praxis to take place, at least two constitutive elements are required so that a true relation can arise: the music and the listener. This also means, however, that a distinction between those two must remain. Here, we come across a fundamental difference between the musical and the mystical experience: while both are triggered by the appeal of otherness, the latter promotes a loss of the self, a complete indulgence of the individual consciousness in the other realm, whereas the former—the musical experience—is possible only as long as the listener does *not* disappear in it.

In order to experience music as meaningful, therefore, we need to focus on the way it unfolds *in time*. Here, Jerrold Levinson's provocative concept of 'concatenationism' is insightful: when we listen to music, we usually do not focus explicitly on its large-scale forms but rather listen to it 'in the moment': "*Musical understanding* certainly involves neither aural grasp of a large span of music as a whole, nor intellectual grasp of large-scale connections between parts; understanding music is centrally a matter of apprehending individual bits of music and immediate progressions from bit to bit."[17] We move along with the music and hear how every motif or gesture relates to the preceding one, preparing the way for further material. Yet, if the listener stops paying attention to the music—she might be too much carried by it, losing herself in a state of ecstasy, or simply lose her interest or be distracted—one of the two constituting elements of the listening practice disappears. Thus, it would no longer make sense to speak of a true relation since there is no 'I' to follow the music's development in time. In this case, the music loses its meaning. This is not to say, however, that the mystical experience in which the 'I' temporarily disappears as an individual cannot be meaningful, but there is a sense of the word 'meaning' that cannot be attributed to whatever the mystical experience grants us while it does seem to be present in the musical experience. The meaningfulness of the mystical experience, so it seems, is still connected to the idea that it is a rewarding enterprise, that it is no waste of time but a practice in function of our physical or spiritual well-being. In the musical experience, though,

[17] Jerrold Levinson, *Music in the Moment*, Ithaca/London: Cornell University Press, 2007, 13 (emphasis in original).

we feel that another, more autonomous aspect of meaning comes into play: something completely divorced from all notions of usefulness. Music is said to have meaning in a way that cannot be recuperated by a utilitarian logic, cannot be understood as a way to improve our mental state. Rather, it is felt to exist in its own right, as something that we receive from the music without being supposed to do anything further with it.

The exact opposite seems to happen in the case of what we could call the phenomenon of 'appropriation' of music: when we hear a certain piece of music too often, when we are confronted with it constantly or listen to it many times in a row it gradually loses its meaning, at least to a certain extent. The music, then, gets gradually absorbed or appropriated by the listener until it dissolves into redundancy and no longer seduces the listener to seriously want to engage in it. Here, we find a ground for an aesthetic maxim that is commonly used to discriminate great art from that which is merely good: the greater a work is, the more we can listen to it or look at it without becoming bored and losing our attention. Great works of art seem to be more immune to this particular kind of appropriation since they continue to provide us with new impressions, new elements to discover—their material presence seems almost inexhaustible and keeps us eager to want to hear or see them again. Such works contain a promise of ever new realms to be explored by our ears or eyes and never seem to lose their appeal of otherness. They refuse to give up their independence, regardless of our appropriating tendencies and thus succeed in saving the 'magic', even when they are fully exposed. In short, in order for musical meaning to emerge not only the listener must be in the game, the music itself must also remain present as an eternal external.

So, if we agree that this is the structure of the listening experience—a balanced, intentional relation between the listener and the music—can we now answer the narrow question and point out *what* it is that we experience as being so wonderfully granted to us and that we tend to call music's meaning? This seems to remain problematic, if not impossible at all—it is in this sense that we must understand, I believe, Vladimir Jankélévitch's famous claim that music expresses the 'Ineffable'.[18] Does

[18] Vladimir Jankélévitch. *La Musique et l'Ineffable*, Paris : Editions du Seuil, 1983.

this mean, however, that after all there is no real meaning to be found in the music beyond a general 'feeling' of meaningfulness that we experience when relating to it in the sense pointed out by Nozick? I think there is more meaning in music than that, even though we cannot paraphrase it: whenever we relate to a concrete instance of music we do not only feel that we are engaging in a meaningful activity but we truly feel that the music *has* a meaning. We do not merely enjoy the liberating force of grasping a part of the otherwise ungraspable dimension of otherness that we seek to relate to but we tend to experience this otherness in its material concreteness as being the bearer of a *particular* meaning, even though it is inseparable from the tones themselves. I believe, moreover, that this peculiar phenomenon, which I have called 'the emergence of musical meaning', lies at the basis of the idea that the meaning of music 'resides' somewhere, waiting to be discovered by the listener. However, as we have seen, treating musical meaning as a separate entity risks turning the music itself into some sort of code to be cracked, eventually reducing it to a disposable means to an end.

Recapitulating, an approach based on static concepts that are detached from the context of lived experience—a metaphysical approach, in other words—is bound to miss out on something essential about music. By formulating the question so that it rigidly asks *what* the music means or *where* it resides, we disregard the dynamic character of the listening experience and it becomes impossible to understand how musical meaning can ever come into being. By asking the wrong questions we embark on a never-ending quest, looking for the location of meaning as an elusive content. A phenomenological understanding of the musical experience, on the other hand, which recognizes it as a descendant of the mystical experience—even if quite remote—reveals musical meaning as an ever-changing phenomenon that is thoroughly singular and highly concrete since it is a consciously lived experience *of* time *in* time. Through relating to it we come to experience the music as having a meaning, as long as we remain aware of its otherness. Moreover, since the emergence of musical meaning does not take place outside the boundaries of daily life but instead inscribes itself radically within our lives as yet another way of relating to the outside world, it is, after all, no wonder that we care so much for music.

References

01. Charlton, David, ed., *E.T.A. Hoffmann's Musical Writings: Kreisleriana; The Poet and the Composer; Music Criticism*, trans. M. Clarke, Cambridge: Cambridge University Press, 2003.

02. Combarieu, Jules, *La musique et la magie. Etude sur les origines populaires de l'art musical, son influence et sa fonction dans les sociétés*, Paris: Alphonse Picard et fils, 1909.

03. Danto, Arthur, 'The Philosophical Disenfranchisement of Art', *Grand Street*, Vol. 4, No. 3 (Spring, 1985), 171-189.

04. Danto, Arthur, *Beyond the Brillo Box*, Berkeley: University of California Press, 1992.

05. Hanslick, Eduard, *On the Musically Beautiful. A Contribution Towards the Revision of the Aesthetics of Music*, trans. Geoffrey Payzant, Indianapolis: Hackett, 1986.

06. Huxley, Aldous, *The Doors of Perception and Heaven and Hell*, New York: Harper & Row, 1990.

07. Jankélévitch, Vladimir, *La Musique et l'Ineffable*, Paris: Editions du Seuil, 1983.

08. Kant, Immanuel, *Critique of Judgement,* trans. J. H. Bernard, New York: Hafner Press, 1951.

09. Kivy, Peter, *Introduction to a Philosophy of Music*, Oxford: Clarendon Press, 2002.

10. Levinson, Jerrold, *Music in the Moment*, Ithaca / London: Cornell University Press, 2007.

11. Moyaert, Paul, *Iconen en beeldverering, godsdienst als symbolische praktijk*, Amsterdam: Sun, 2007.

12. Nietzsche, Friedrich, *The Birth of Tragedy,* trans. Clifton P. Fadiman, New York: Dover Publications, 1995.

13. Nozick, Robert, *Philosophical Explanations*, Cambridge: Harvard University Press, 1981.

14. Plato, *Republic,* tarns. Benjamin Jowett, New York: Barnes & Noble Classics, 2004.

9

Bāuls, Mystic Minstrels of Bengal

Builders of a New Tomorrow in the Realm of Global Music

Dr. Sanchita Choudhury
Dept. of Humanities and Social Sciences
Indian Institute of Technology, Kharagpur

A Bāul[1] is conventionally known for its captivating music, performance and enigmatic life style. It is a sect, a philosophy and a folk music of Bengal. The follower of the Bāul philosophy is a Bāul himself. In this paper, I shall bring to light the essence of Baul philosophy, their historical background in short, their 'otherness' in the society apart from this partial understanding about them and most importantly their onward journey towards a new tomorrow through their music. Although a spiritual seeker, a Bāul is quite often unaware of the subtlety and nuances of their own philosophy. He is most often not very conversant with the written texts. A Bāul's pursuit for higher truth is in terms of realizations through the spiritual practices instead of the usual conceptualization of the theoretical tenets. The simple ways of understanding and conceptualizing profound thoughts are manifested through Bāul songs that are most often composed spontaneously as an outburst of intoxicating emotions.

---

[1] Bāul is a vagabond, mendicant, but iconoclastic folk sect who is spread over different districts of greater Bengal, West Bengal and Bangladesh. Bāuls are a clan of mystic minstrels *who* ideally live on alms and lead an itinerant life. They live a distinct way of life committed to an esoteric religious cult in the social and cultural context of Bengal.

Bāul is a vagabond, mendicant, iconoclastic folk sect of Bengal. Etymologically, the word 'Bāul' resonates with the Sanskrit word '*vāyu*', or '*bāyu*' in Bāngla that means air. (Tagore 188)[2] 'Bāul' is a synonym of the word '*byakula*' or over anxious, and '*ākul*', which denotes one who is over anxious. However, Shashibhushan Das Gupta is of the view that the word 'Bāul' can be derived in three ways: (i) From the Sanskrit word *vātula*, which means 'infected with wind disease'. (ii) From the Sanskrit word *vyākula*, which means irresistible or over anxious. (iii) From the Arabic word *āuliyā*, this means friend or devotee (83-84). With the Bāuls being associated with Islam in some ways, there is no reason etymologically, to ignore this third possibility.

Charles Capwell in *The Music of the Bāuls of Bengal* states, "They are the products of the cross current of several forces- Tāntric or Sahajiyā Buddhism, Vaishnava- Sahajiyā and Indo-Persian Sufism." The Bāul, as an independent sect, has been influenced by several faiths and series of cults like Buddhist Tāntricism, Brahmanic Tāntricism, Vaishnava- Sahajiyā and Sufi-ism. Researchers and eminent scholars like Bhattacharya (1364 B. S), Das Gupta (1962), Dimock (1966) and Chakrabortee (1980) have illustrated and exhaustively elaborated this aspect in the form of textual analysis in their respective books. Dimock comments, "[...] the Bāuls are fitting hybrids, the Vaishnava, Sahajiyā, and Sufi strains yield beauty, sympathy, and strength. From the Vaishnavas, and from the Sufis, come the Bāul vision of the warmth and humanness and love of God. From the Sahajiyās come their convictions of His compelling immediacy" (189). In *Obscure Religious Cults*, Shashibhushan Das Gupta, while describing their religious philosophy, depicts one of the important features of Bāuls. He points out that those who have come from a Hindu background were highly influenced by Vaishnavism and those of Islam brought with them many Sufi distinctiveness, although their ultimate goal remains the same- 'mystic conception of divine love'. By defying established faiths and religions; society and social strictures; this sect defines its own identity. This is why he points out that in general they are identified

[2] The Sanskrit 'v' becomes 'b' in the eastern part of Bihar, Bengal, Assam and Orissa, and, thus, the Sanskrit intervocalic constant is often dissolved.

as "[…] somewhat strange people, peculiar in their customs, habits and practices."(160-63)

Bāul philosophy questions the essentialist notions of Islam and Hinduism. Both from the textual and contextual evidences it appears that they are very unconventional in their social and religious behaviour, and prefer to live independently. The idea of human beings differentiated on the basis of caste and beliefs, torments a pensive Bāul. Lālon Shāhi or Lālon Shāi sings, "*Lālon bole jāter ki roop, dekhlāmnā ei nojore*" (Lālon says I fail to see how a caste looks like). Rabindranath Tagore, in *Religion of Man,* covers the wide spectrum of Bāul philosophy- its musical cultures and life style that embraces universal aspect of human religion. He vividly delineates the aesthetic expression of the people through music and poetry too, "[…] what struck me in this simple song was a religious expression that was neither grossly concrete, full of crude details, nor metaphysical in its rarefied transcendentalism […]. It spoke of an intense yearning of the heart for the Divine which is in Man and not in the temple, or scriptures, in images and symbols."(110) Jāhan, a Bāul, when questioned by researcher Sudhir Chakrabarti regarding their apathy towards social and religious institution, he bursts out in remonstration, spontaneously singing- "*Bāmun bole bhinno jāti/ Srishti ki koren prakriti? /Tobe keno jātir bojjāti koro ekhon bhāi* […] *Bedānte āche kothāy āmarā dekhi nāi.*"(Brahmins claim themselves to be a different caste/ Are they not created by *prakriti?*[3] /Then O brother, why are you doing mischief in the name of caste? […] We have never evinced all these in the Vedānta).[4] According to the Bāuls, human beings cannot be differentiated based on caste, or confined to particular human-made social boundaries. Bāuls are vagabonds who lead and live their life valorizing human birth and human identity. *Ādi kavi* Chandidās[5] sings, "*Shobār upore mānush satya, tāhār upore nāi*" (The ultimate truth is human being, and none else is above them). This is one of the strong reasons behind their social ostracism. The society that differentiated

[3] women/nature

[4] Upanishad

[5] Born in 1408 CE approximately refers to a medieval poet of Bengal who is known for his love peoms on Radha and Krishna and lyrical *Srikrishna Kirtan* (Songs in praise of Lord Sri Krishna)

human beings on the basis of their faith and lineage, could not accept the magnanimous humanism of the Bāuls.

Earlier Bāuls were found over several districts of greater Bengal[6]- Birbhum, Malda, Bankura, Midnapur in West Bengal and Kushtia, Meherpur, Chuadanga, Pabna, Jessore, Faridpur, Jhenidah in Bangladesh. These days, however, they have expanded over many more districts of Bengal, India and abroad. Ideally, Bāuls settle far from mainstream society. But, unlike their predecessors, contemporary Bāuls prefer suburban locales to rustic fringes. *Sanyāsi*[7] Bāuls, especially reside in *ākhadās*[8] or *āshram*[9] situated away from the social habitat.

Bāul philosophy emphasizes the awakening of the *moner mānush*[10] through renunciation and discipline. A true Bāul stays miles away from material accumulations and possessions like land, name and fame, pride, ego and alike. According to this philosophy, accumulation of material possessions strengthens the urge to achieve 'more' thereby derailing the *sādhaka*[11] from the track that leads to his/her goal. The path of realizing the *moner mānush* leads to a plane of transcendentalism. It is therefore beyond the reach of a *bhogi*[12]. Living an itinerant life is an inevitable necessity for a Bāul in quest of his inner soul. As a spiritual seeker, a Bāul's way of living is instinctively simple, ascetic, vagabond and not premeditated. Even today Bāuls are seen singing and begging from door to door, in public transports like buses and local trains, in public places like cultural or heritage parks, *melā*[13] or *machchaba*[14]. In an interview with Parvathy Bāul, she told me that during her 'Bāulhood' days, she used to beg in local trains along with her *guru mā*[15] for alms. In order to lead a simple life like a true Bāul, she had to renounce all materialistic

---

[6] West Bengal and Bangladesh

[7] Monk

[8] A socio-cultural institution in Bangladesh and Eastern India; spiritual Retreat for some sects

[9] A Retreat

[10] The inner soul or self

[11] Spiritual seeker

[12] Hedonist; one who seeks material comfort

[13] Fair

[14] Celebration for a spiritual cause

[15] Preceptor

benefits including the comfort of a bed in order to surrender herself at the feet of the Supreme. Many reputed Bāuls singers like Purna Dās Bāul, Kārtik Dās Bāul and Goshto Gopāl Dās began their spiritual journey from 'something' to 'nothing', and eventually be spotted by connoisseurs of music while begging in local trains and localities.

Amidst the serious hurdles to establishing their identity as a clan, Bāuls strived hard to retain their simple living style to finally unite with the Supreme. Their state of 'otherness' remained ingrained in them eventually consigning the Bāuls to the fringes of the society. Their practices and religious performances were ostracized in spite of their indifference towards immediate social events. However, they continued to be seekers of the eternal bliss through their distinct path of mysticism that finally leads to *mukti*[16] and the final union with the inner soul or the *moner mānush*. Longing for the *moner mānush* actually evolves from *manqué* or 'lack' in Jacques Lacan's expression. It is the initial identity crisis due to social castration that drives a Bāul desperately towards the fulfillment, that is, realization of the *moner mānush*.

Bāuls are known to common people through their enigmatic, lively and bewitching songs that are the index of their yearning heart in look for their *moner mānush*. Their lyrics exude an authentic essence of mysticism, philanthropic philosophy and symbolic overtone, although simplicity in the text apparently baffles the listeners many a time. Chandidās encapsulates the essence of his feelings when he sings, "*Ghar kainu bāhir/ Bāhir kainu ghar/ Par kainu āpon/ Āpon kainu par*" (I have made the world my niche/ And my home the world, / I have made 'others' my own people, / And my own people as 'others'). Rāj Krishna Khyāpā, an eminent Bāul singer, mocks at the world divided into castes and sects. He says, "*Yābat uchcha nich bichār/ Kara tābat bhrānti tomār/ Tattva jnāne sab ekākār*" (So long as you judge people in terms of high and low, you are deluded; all are the same to one who knows reality).

Bāul songs, simple in theme and words but exuding a subtle and an enigmatic essence through sporadic use of philosophical metaphors and metonymies, form an important genre of folk music in Bengal. These songs are now popular not only outside West Bengal or Bangladesh but

[16] Salvation

also in the Western World and are an important part of the folk-culture industry. Bāul *Samrāt*[17] Purna Dās Bāul, in an interview with *The Telegraph* 5 December 1982, Colour Magazine, said: "You know, Bob Dylan is a sort of Bāul. And so are the hippies…All over the world we have met Bāuls." The image of Bāuls as Bengali hippies dominates the media and is assiduously fed back to the potential patrons for the sake of popularity of the clan and music by an increasing number of cultural brokers who export Bāul singers to foreign countries like U.S.A, U.K, Japan, France, Italy, Russia and so on. A community that thrives only for the realization of its philosophy- union with The Supreme or the *moner mānush*, Bāuls win the hearts of people by mesmerizing listeners through their songs. Music, an effortless enigmatic medium of expression, is Bāuls' signature and the prime medium of communication with the world. Their traditional media of communication are exchange of ideas through songs, *machchabā* and *melā* other than the routine exchange of ideas and creations in the *akhadās*--- a platform of intermixing within and outside the Bāul society.

Bāul songs are however, not merely mimesis of 'raw' emotions. Emotions are rendered and made an integral part of the *sādhaka's* esoteric practices. That is, Bāul music is not solely dependent on emotions. Spontaneity of emotions outbursts from a spiritually charged soul. Aristotle[18] believed that music plays a pivotal role in the process of emotional 'purification'. Itinerant living style of Bāuls is one of the major reasons to consider music as an integral part of their life and *sādhanā*[19]. Bāul *sādhakas* believe that mere emotional renderings do not help transcend the soul. It is one's realisation through prescribed *sādhana*, that one composes music of the soul. That is why a *sādhaka* sings—"*Nā mojile hoyna bhajan, /pābe kire nirākāre*." (Unless one is seasoned as a spiritual seeker devotion cannot keep going, / and one cannot attain the ultimate stage of formless salvation). It is the union of

[17] Emperor

[18] "Aristotle on Aesthetics," 1902, Encyclopedia: http://webcache.googleusercontent.com/ search?q=cache:IM0cF35EtMsJ www.1902encyclopedia.com/A/AES/aesthetics-09.html+Aristotle+music+emotional+%E2%80%98purification%E2%80%99&cd=9&hl=en&ct=clnk&gl=in (Web. 1 Nov 2010).

[19] Spiritual disciplined practice

emotion, intelligence, logic and *sādhanā* that brings out the real essence of the Bāul philosophy, which is also a folk song of Bengal.

Itinerant life style of Bāuls and the passion to preserve their indigenous culture are the possible reasons behind the use of accompanying light-weighed instruments like *Ektārā*, *Bāmā*, *Gābgubi*, *Nupur*, *Dotārā*; these are the cult-instruments of Bāuls. An *Ektārā* is a single string musical instrument, which is made of wood, bamboo, splits, piece of tanned animal skin and string. One string is attached to a hollow circular box at the bottom on one hand and with the meeting place of two bamboo splits on the other. Fingers of the performer play it. *Bāmā* is an earthen hollow musical instrument. One side of it is covered by a circular piece of tanned animal skin. It is a percussion accompanied in the rhythmic songs. The singer strikes on the circular skin part by the fist of the left hand to obtain a uniform beat of sound. *Gābgubi* is made of a wooden hollow box of six inches height with a piece of circular tanned skin attached to the box at the bottom and with a pot of brass metal at the top. In order to produce a jingling sound as a rhythmic accompaniment, Bāuls wear jingling anklets called *nupur* and dance while performing their songs. Some of the Bāuls, these days, sing to the accompaniment of non-traditional musical instruments like *Dotārā*, harmonium, flutes and violins etc. However the cult-instruments are used even if the non-traditional instruments are liberally played to make the presentation more gorgeous and indigenous.

Postmodern music tends to dissolve structural and cultural criteria eventually giving shape to hybrid musical varieties. Music evolving in this milieu operates on a multitude of levels. On the one hand, it endeavours to retain the aesthetic flavour that captures the mood variations and emotions encompassing a complex amalgam of religious, mythological and temporal references. On the other hand it reflects the pulse of time through progressive improvisation in dynamic form. It is difficult to categorize such musical developments and label them as a particular form. Subjective conclusions drawn; either by common masses or connoisseurs of a particular locale or musical faculty regarding its etymological existence, lead to further complications in the formation of a genre. But the establishment of an independent genre of music depends on the acceptance of people and the test of time. Conceptualising generic identities and relating their importance in musical life, Fabian Holt points out: "It is [...] a tool with which culture industries and national governments regulate the circulation of vast fields of music. It is a major force in canons of educational institutions, cultural hierarchies, and decisions about censorship and funding. The apparatus of corporate music is thoroughly organized in generic and market categories."(3)

Understanding genres, sub-genres and sub-subgenres with visibly correct connotations leads to getting into the generated web of styles with a temporal sense. Holt says: "The network of genre can be understood from the perspective that the genre is a constellation of styles connected by a sense of tradition. These aspects distinguish genres from marketing categories and labels because it has a more stable existence in cultures of musical specializations among musicians, listener, critics, pedagogues, and others." (18) The traditional and cultural aspects that pertain to a particular style quite stably for a period of time eventually develop into a genre. However opinions vary from person to person regarding the concept of style and genre. Categories like 'race records', 'top 40', or 'chill-out music' is not understood as genres in Holt's model. For that matter Holt refuses to consider 'mainstream pop' as a genre since he thinks it is defined as *ex negative* and is mainly based on a star culture with its different social context. Similarly veterans in the field of folk music of Bengal, especially Bāul singers, think that random experiments neither do justice to the Bāul philosophy and Bāul music. Nor do these ventures satisfy the definite purpose; these are merely an arbitrary attempt to re-define a form already popular in Bengal.

Experiment, practice and performance of Fusion Bāul music in the main stream of music industry have been in vogue since the early nineties. Although exploration in the realm of fusion Bāul music was initiated by Purna Dās Bāul and Bob Dylan way back in 60s and carried forward in the 70s by the pioneers of Bānglā Band '*Mohiner Ghoraguli*', its socio-cultural significance has been different at different intervals in time. A section of Bāul singers of the present generation gladly welcome a liberal infusion of musical elements of other streams of music and the member of this group is increasing in number day by day. However, there are a large number of amateur Bāul singers who readily stoop to compromise with the demands in the music market. Gentlemen or *bhadralok* amateur Bāuls or Non-Bāul folk musicians or rock artistes gladly experiment with Bāul music with a flavour of World music that generates a mixed response. Fusion music and World music are two independent genres, but very few practicing musicians are aware of their technicalities and intricacies that must be understand for a musician to be able to create a palatable concoction- Fusion music. Practicing this music with a touch of World music is part of their random experiments. I have come across many such successful artists who have neither a sound grounding in Bāul music nor a basic understanding of Western nor World Music but are regular performers of fusion folk, especially Fusion Bāul. They are, in fact, a big name in the music industry probably due to their public acceptance, especially among *bhadralok* class and foreign music lovers. Indrajit Dey, a practicing musician of rock and fusion music, claims that world and fusion music are often misinterpreted. He says: "Every fusion music is a kind of *WORLD MUSIC* [...] but every *WORLD* music is not a fusion music." Ashok Ranade points out the difficulty that folk music underwent to establish itself as an independent genre due to the lack of a concrete structure *per se,* which further hints at the practical impediments and challenges that fusion-folk is facing today to ascertain its status as an independent genre and class. Holt stresses the importance of genre but simultaneously apprehends the limitations of a structured genre. He tells that genres are important as they provide the starting points of the eclectic fusion process, but it is less clear to what extent musical results can still be attached to a genre. He also points out that live performances are usually more eclectic than studio recordings as CDs have to be sold in significant numbers, to this reason, while the producers of music are interested in fusion, their recipients appear to be more interested in purism. (Holt 31) These factors compel us to ponder, rethink and research the status of fusion-Bāul music, which is criticized for being a structure less bohemian experiment instead of possessing musicality. It is yet to be included in the canonized dictionary of music. However, one has to thoughtfully and critically investigate the reason behind the potential claim of this music to an independent genre and not a sub genre of popular music. A fusion package, with a careful infusion of musical pulse effect, hip-hop elements, jazz, blue, psychedelic matrix cannot be marginalized as a sub-genre of a popular music.

Established and popular genres frequently contest with emerging or new genres with similar patterns. Many critics are of the view that generic evolution is much like a relay race. But there are times when this analogy fails. Heather Dubrow points out the caveat offered by critics about the transgression and overlapping of genres: "The image of relay race suggested by some critics for generic evolution is apt in certain cases but not all. While a genre is still living it may compete with others that fill the same functions. Two genres may enjoy the relationship of genre and counter-genre while both are active, with one of the two taking over many elements of the other when it decays." (114) Bewilderment and ambiguity breed complications while determining the status or validity of forms of art. Bāul music and fusion Bāul music are similar in many aspects but intentionally different in certain perspectives. Although fusion Bāul music began its journey as a subset of Bāul music, it claims to be an independent form according to some practicing musicians. Upal Sen Gupta, the lead vocalist of Chandrabindu or Tatai, the bass guitarist, of Athoi, thinks that 'creation through fusion' generates a new concept that captures the authentic essence of time. Bāul music reflects its profundity through words carefully picked to deceive the ignorant and non-initiated masses but still conveys, to some degree, the illusions and truth of life. Almost every contemporary musician has unanimously agreed that it is difficult to experiment with indigenous music, especially with Bāul songs with their subtle composition and typical Bāul *gāyaki.*[20]

Musical transfusion might be in vogue, but capricious adventure might be dangerous in a sense that it increases the chances of the decontextualisation of a piece of art like Bāul songs without a planned purpose or vision. While discussing this issue with some Bāul singers, I learnt about their anxiety and apprehensions about this 'bohemian' musical journey. Many of them think that Bāul music will live as long as human civilization since the journey that began centuries back cannot end abruptly or deform and stoop to earn a few more years of life. However, musicians like Vikramjeet alias Tuki of Krosswindz, Bonny of Oikyotān, Upal of Chandrabindu, Tatai of Athoi, or music director Indrajeet Dey think concur that experiments and improvisations are made not to

[20] Singing style

degrade Bāul music or the inherent profound thoughts in Bāul songs but to attune it with present needs by building a structure on the foundation of traditional Bāul music. Chirag Sutar, while depicting Tanmoy Bose's experiments on Bāul music in his article, writes: "Speaking about what drove him to this music, Bose says," I could find a connection between Folk, Jazz, Indian classical music paired with the timeless philosophies of the Bāul music. However, it's unfortunate that people are not aware of our indigenous genres. "[...] Bāuls constitute both a syncretic religious sect and have a strong musical tradition for spiritual expression [...]. Bose was incited to do this album since his experiments with Bāul music with his band Taal Tantra were well appreciated [...]. His band Taal Tantra features Andreas Weiser (percussionist), Kai Bruckner (guitar), Max Hughes (bassist), Tilmann Dehnhardt (saxophone) and Bāul musicians with a dotara and a traditional dhaki. Music aficionados who have attended their performances regard it as one of the best examples of fusion music in recent times. For this album, Bose has collaborated with Bāul musicians namely Lakshman Das Bāul, Krishna Das Bairagya, Kartick Das Bāul and Bangaldesh's popular Bāul singer Anusheh Anadil." Sutar also points out that "The album is unique for one more reason – the instrumentals are allowed to have their own life as majority of the songs featuring on the album go well beyond seven minutes."

A conspicuous development that contests the earlier established conventions is visible. Instruments, which were earlier typecast as accompanying musical tools, are widely played both independently and as accompanying tools. Some indigenous and folk music instruments are modernized and modified to meet with the challenge posed by time. Musicians are extremely excited due to the pervasive revolution, which seems to have demystified earlier perceptions about music and musical technicalities. Stereotypes are no more in vogue; rather the ambitious audience of this millennium finds a meaningful thought in a new garb to be more satisfying. Nandini Guha writes about such musicians in "New Age Notes"[21]. She begins, "Ace percussionist Bickram Ghosh was tired of being drowned out by other louder instruments when he was

[21] Graphiti, *The Telegraph*, 22 August 2010

playing in fusion concerts. There was no way his *tablā*[22] could compete with sounds being produced on stage by his fellow musicians. To get around the problem Ghosh added an instrument called a handsonic- it's an electric hand drum- to be played alongside his *tablā*." Ghosh says: "I was looking for a punchy, racy sound. So I used the handsonic, which I picked up from the US." Nandini Guha summarizes: "Ghosh and the other musicians are trying to give a new twist to fusion music with the electric versions of their instruments." Musicians like Bikram Ghosh include Rajesh Vaidhya with his electric *veena*, Prattyush Banerjee with his *jyotidhwani*, Purbayan Chatterjee and his version of the electric guitar and Snehasis Majumdar with his doubled necked electric mandolin. These modified instruments help produce certain sounds that resonate with time. Prattyush Banerjee says: "Because of the long sustained notes, I can play the alaap of a Hindustani classical composition better on the electrified instrument. The *taan*, *gamak* and *tihai* also sound better with the electric instruments," Ghosh asserts that he uses the handsonic for the bass guitar tone mostly during fusion concerts. He adds: "This combination creates a dense groove which, in fact, is the backbone of my sound in albums like *Rhythmscape* or *Electro Classical*," Vaidhya seems to be happy with the 'fast pace' that can be easily played in Electro Classical with the help of his modified electric *veena*. Even a veteran musician like *sarod* maestro Pandit Tejendra Narayan Majumdar is confident about the modulation made possible through 'electrified instruments' although he is still not very confident about its full-fledged execution of a complete *raga*. The consequence of this dynamic experimentation is their instant reception by the new generation. This is one of the major reasons why musicians do not hesitate to use electrified instruments in fusion music. On being asked about his recent music album *Electro Musicians Classical*, Ghosh says: "I realized sometimes back that a large number of Indians didn't attend classical concerts. They missed the familiar sound of pop and rock concerts. This sound was constituted by the electric tonality of instruments and also the grooviness of popular music." Musicians creating Bāul fusions are tempted to create precision, and, therefore, generously use these instruments in their creative musical adventure.

[22] Percussion instrument played in India

This evolving form of Bāul music with heterogeneous musical elements from across the globe poses an inevitable question and raises suspicion and reservations about the validity of such experiments due to unorganized and often whimsical improvisations. The audience or listeners, in general, take pleasure in building a mental frame of a particular genre or form of music they already appreciate, and in order to comprehend that better they carry the mental frame for future reference. They often feel cheated, with some of the impregnable intricacies in the creation, when subjected to performances and shows that do not match with the mental map they happily carry with them. For example, improvisations in "*Dil ki doya hoynā*" by Paban Das Bāul and experimentations of Athoi, a musical band based in Kolkata, with one of the very popular songs of Lālon Fakir "*Āmār bārir kāche ārshi nogor*" neither match in a greater sense with that nor do they abide by any integral code of music. In fact, it is difficult to identify "*Āmār bārir kāche ārshi nogor*" as one of Lālon Fakir's songs unless informed in advance. Two popular Bāul songs, "*Nāchite nāchite shundori komolā*" by Chandrani of Krosswindz and "*Meye shorbonāshi,*" by Dohār manifest as different musical presentations although both claim to have made a concoction of Bāul music and music of the world around giving it a final form of Bāul fusion music. Musicians are often tempted to add musical flavours liberally from across the world and develop what is called fusion music, and therein lie the objections of listeners who do not find any resemblance between the people and groups/bands making such music. Moreover these changes that do not reflect the essence of the soil only disappoint the listener. Thus, the consequence as evinced till now is that Bāul music is in a state of crisis. In the name of preserving this dying indigenous music of Bengal, that is Bāul music, rich in many aspects, some musicians carelessly, playfully and randomly experiment with its musical characteristics there by giving it a deformed shape.

Change is inevitable in any musical genre. Musicians across the world have explored different terrains of music and socio-cultural aspects pertaining to music in order to create new forms or upgraded version of traditional music. Diachronic studies and analyses indicate that a form of music changes over the years and emerges into a new form, sometimes surpassing the existing one. Musicians, who are aware of the profundity of Bāul philosophy and have an in-depth knowledge of Bāul music, can perhaps venture into such experimentation and create a mutant that resonates with the traditional form. Even for a person like Mimlu Sen, who has been traveling, performing and living with the mystic minstrels for decades, this has been a difficult venture. In the Epilogue of her book *Bāul Sphere* she states her dilemma: "Should we bend our rhythms to hiphop and break dance tracks? Continue to explore Mandingue melodies from Mali and jazz rhythms? Take our musical encounters with the fabulous desert musicians of Rajasthan towards an album? How do we cross over the grid of rules and regulations, laws and by-laws which govern copyright, and, in fact, existence itself in Europe? [...] Should we drop all this...? Should we go to Bāul country in Birbhum and create a Bāul mahotsava on our newly acquired land in the village of Lohagarh near the forests, which border the Kopai River? Do we abandon our fantastic shuttle between Europe and India? Can we do both?" (279) In many instances we find that people claim such improvisation as an effect of globalization. But Mimlu Sen, in a different context, admits, "Instead of drawing our disparate worlds closer together, globalization seems to have had the opposite effect on our lives."(278) It is now evident that playful experiments have been deluding people instead of forming a new beginning. These spurious works baffle people to such an extent that they eventually fail to distinguish between authentic and erratic experimentation; between fusion and musical concoction without any definite objective.

New experiments and explorations have signaled an accelerated alteration of Bāul music, which seems to have been deeply influenced by the rich tapestry of musical genres in Bengal like the plaintive folk melody, *Kirtan*[23], boatmen songs and many more. However, Bāul songs, as mentioned earlier, are no longer restricted to the region of Bengal or India nor has the process of exploration restricted itself to a geographical periphery. Bāul song, which is traditionally a melismatic solo accompanied by chordophones like *ektārā* or *dotārā* and

[23] Kirtans are Hindu Vaishnav devotional songs which employ an "improvisatory technique known as akhar (textural elaboration on the existing words of a poem), [which] lengthens the original song into a more complex structure" (Saaduddin 1980:114).

membanophones like *khamak*, has been sung in a non-traditional and non-stereotypical manner to evoke the flavour of time and importance of the result generated out of musical adventure for the past few decades. Change is envisaged in every aspect of the singing style and mode of presentation of Bāul songs. With an objective to popularize Bāul songs, musicians have opted for fast rhythms. They have preferred fast triplets/ couplets or reggae beats to medium paced 4/6 beats or slow 8 beats rhythmic cycle. Some Bāul songs (Bangladeshi Bāul songs especially), which are metrically fluid, non-rhythmic or slow paced melodies with long held notes in the higher octave, have been completely transformed into a rock fusion. *Thakte pār ghātāte tumi pārer nāiyā*, a slow tempo Bāul song of Bangladesh originally sung in a slow 8 beat rhythmic cycles similar to a typical *bhātiyali* river/boatman song, has been sung by Khalid Hassan Milu in fast 6 beats rhythmic cycle with occasional improvisations. Another vibrant example is a popular Bāul song *Tomāy Hrid majhāre rākhbo chere debona* that delineates the ecstasy of the Rādhā Krishna romance in a *Kirtan* style of singing. Babukishan das Bāul, Paban Das Bāul, Tarak Das Bāul, Satyaki Khyepa Bāul and many other Bāul singers have sung this song for many years. However, a distinct style of presentation cannot be overlooked when music bands of the new millennium like Blue Eyes, Sandhān and others perform the same song many times in a conspicuously different singing style.

The acquisition of status in the domain of music is spontaneous and inevitable, although many such nascent musical attempts wither within a course of time. The possibility of acquiring the status of a genre becomes bleak for many musical adventures due to critics and researcher's reservations about the status of Bāul fusion music uncommon. In spite of their unstructured patterns, patches and heterogeneity, Bāul *bhāva*[24] cannot be overlooked in most of the new creations. Their apparent or imperceptible dissimilarities should not be suppressed in order to establish a genre/ sub genre or simply a musical status among the masses. In the disorganized musical frame, lies an inordinately musical structure that reverberates with time, that is, they strive to capture the taste of the mass through their musical expedition. Impression of time

[24] Emotion

is inevitable in artistic creations, and hence the present amalgamation in the era of globalization.

The *rasa*[25] and *bhāva* emanating from a musical creation determine its intrinsic musical genre in spite of the musical grandeur and heterogeneity. So long as the Bāul *bhāva* subsists amicably with exotic musical elements, music seems palatable for the mass. The addition of elements of 'other' music destroys the Bāul flavour only when the attempt is desperate and whimsical. Practitioners of fusion music indulge in heterogeneous creations and as a result a musical collage like Bāul fusion generates a homogenous structure within its heterogeneity. Bāul *rasa* in Bāul-fusion establishes a genre with a different profile.

In Indian aesthetics, *rasa* plays a pivotal role in determining an art form. According to Sneh Pandit: "An object which does not contain *rasa* cannot be classed in the category of an art work, and no experience without it can be called aesthetic [...]. In other words, *rasa* as a quality of the art object and of the aesthetic consciousness could synthesize both aspects and offer a point of reconciliation." (32) While referring to Bullough's concept on identification, she says: "Identification according to him is the natural state of mind wherein the self is identified with what it feels. The introduction of distance alters this state of identity by filtering the relation between the self and its feeling of its personal character." She further adds: "The act of identity arises out of the capacity to detach oneself from passive and blind impulses, but it is consequently an independent state of mind, constituted no doubt of the ordinary emotional state but transforming this into a new and different kind of experience." (46) The presence of *bhāva* in a consistent degree eventually helps in the process of identification of a particular genre in a particular piece. Bikram Ghosh thinks that expert knowledge of musical genres is essential for experimenting with them to create music. A musician must feel the aesthetic necessity to fuse varied musical elements for producing a desired effect. In a particular context he says: *"Fusion can be the most risky form of music. Ij you don't know how to get different genres together aesthetically, you'll end up making noise, not music. You should be adequately prepared and equipped."*

---

[25] A particular emotion with its distinct aesthetic quality

References

01. Bhattacharya, Mahendra Nath, ed. *Andul Kali Kirtan O Bāul Gitabali*, Andul: Taraprasanna Bhattacharya, 1359 (B.S).
02. Capwell, Charles, *The Music of the Bāuls of Bengal*, Kent Ohio: The Kent State UP, 1986, 34-35, 242.
03. Chakrabartee, Surath Chandra, *Bāuls: The Spiritual Vikings*, Calcutta: Firma KLM, 1980.
04. Chakrabarty, Sudhir, ed. *Gavir Nirjan Pathe*, Calcutta: Ananda, 1989.
05. Das Gupta, Shashibhusan, *Obscure Religious Cult*, Calcutta: Firma KLM. 1946,160-63.
06. Dimock, Edward C., *The Place of the Hidden Moon*, Chicago: 1966, 258.
07. Dubrow, Heather, *Genre*, London: Methuen, 1982.
08. Holt, Fabian, *Genre in Popular Music*, Chicago and London: The U of Chicago P, 2007.
09. Pandit, Sneh, "Rasa as a Principle in Art and Aesthetics," in *An Approach to the Indian Theory of Art and Aesthetic*, New Delhi: Sterling Publishers, 1977, 32.
10. Ranade, Ashok D., "Categories of Music," in *Essays in Indian Ethnomusicology*, New Delhi: Munshiram Manoharlal.1998, 1-25.
11. Sen, Mimlu, *Bāul Sphere*, Noida: Random House India, 2009.
12. Sutar, Chirag, "Tanmoy Bose experiments with Bāul music in new album," *Editorial News*: Radio and Music. Com. 03 Feb 2010 11:13 IST. Web 5 Aug 2010. http://www.radioandmusic.com/content/editorial/news/tanmoy-bose-experiments-with-Bāul-music-new-album
13. Tagore, Rabindranath, *The Religion of Man*, New Delhi: Rupa, 2005.
14. Web. 5 Aug 2010. http://www.newagemusic.nu/tag/bikram-ghosh.
15. You Tube. Babukishan Dās Bāul. Web. 20Aug 2010. http://www.youtube.com/watch?v=hGjsbGTC_2s
16. You Tube. Sātyaki Khyapa Bāul. Web. 20 Aug 2010. http://www.youtube.com/watch?v=gS5E8-4stZY
17. You Tube. Blue Eyes. Web. 20 Aug 2010. http://www.youtube.com/watch?v=QG0RVk1YTnw&feature=related
18. You Tube. Sandhān. Web. 20 August 2010. http://www.youtube.com/watch?v=Ypq-4hAHPFU&feature=related
19. You Tube. Anushesh. Web. 20 August 2010. http://www.youtube.com/watch?v=8m0wOAMNw8Y&feature=related
20. You Tube. "Bonde Māyā". Jackie. Web. 15 Aug 2010. http://www.youtube.com/watch?v=mqlsWDrsCBY&feature=related
21. YouTube. "Moder Kothāi Sono- Bonde Māyā." Shāmimā Alam Chinu. Web. 15 Aug 2010. http://www.youtube.com/watch?v=njK65G9PkSM&feature=related

22. YouTube. Paban Dās Bāul. Web. 30 Aug 2010. http://webcache.googleusercontent.com/search?q=cache:x2b1JMr4ApIJ:www.popmatters.com/pm/review/128139-paban-das-Bāul-music-of-the-honey-gatherers/+media+Bāul&cd=5&hl=en&ct=clnk&gl=in

10

'Art and Mysticism'
Space as an Aesthetic Predicate

Dr. Sebastian Elavathingal
Samanvaya College, India

1. "Space" in Art and Mysticism

In this presentation I would like to explore the relationship of art and mysticism to a dynamic and creative notion of "space." Art and Mysticism have a common interest: both are concerned about the spirit-matter dialectic and hence mediate between the physical and the metaphysical realms of reality. Mysticism may be explained in general terms as a search into the depths of existence which leads to an experience of unity and communion in the world of diversity and multiplicity. It seeks to build a bridge between the physical world of the "many" and the metaphysical world of the "One."

The challenge faced by mystics is to witness a spirit-matter communion and to speak a human language to express this indefinable experience. Artists undertake the task of transforming matter in view of discovering in it or expressing through it experiences or meanings which transcend their works. From this point of view artists and mystics face the same kind of challenge in their efforts. No wonder artists are often mystics and mystics are artists. Their concerns overlap and complement each other. A mystic's vision can be effective and expressive through art. Similarly an artist can produce works which are meaningful and significant through a mystical vision of reality.

2. "Dynamism" of Artworks

We may here explore the history of visual arts like painting and sculpture to identify the tendencies to experiment with the matter-spirit dialectic and to show how artists have been struggling to discover in their works the spiritual and the mystical. History of art is sometimes considered as the history of the Spirit. The Spirit incarnates in history through art, responding to the cultural, religious, social and economic conditions determining the ethos and mentality of the time.

When the spirit-matter dialectic becomes the subject matter of art, art becomes indefinable, changing its form according to the changing times and concerns. Sometimes art goes closer to matter and sometimes closer to the Spirit.[1] Being closer to matter, artworks represent a static, objective consciousness and being closer to the Spirit, artworks witness a dynamic, subjective consciousness. In the ancient Greek art, for example, there was the practice of "imitation" (*mimesis*) which considered resemblance to natural things as the highest artistic value. The artists strived to imitate nature as closely as possible to produce the best resemblance as possible to the original.

The artistic effort to attain the objective quality of the work in its appearance was severely criticised by philosophers like Socrates and Plato. According to Socrates the mimetic artworks of the artists lack vitality and in their lifeless form they capture only the physical aspects of the original. Such works are not acceptable to mature minds. Plato complained about the falsehood of mimetic artworks, since they failed to comprehend reality as it is, since they are replicas of the physical world of shadows and appearances without any reference to the metaphysical world of ideas. Such works of servile copying are deceptive and seductive and therefore harmful to society.

Aristotle proposed a different understanding of imitation in artworks explaining that imitation means representation, and not the copies of natural things. He recognized the creative nature of artistic activity. In Poetics XXVI.6, clarifying the idea of imitation, Aristotle says that the artist imitates not the things as they are, but as they are ought to be. He is not representing the actual but the possible. He emulates the ideal conditions. This notion of imitation implies a dynamic relationship

---

[1] See, Ingo F. Walther, ed. *Art of the 20th Century*, Vols. 1 & 2, Köln: Taschen, 2005.

between the artwork and its signification. In the chapter II of the *Poetics* Aristotle says that the objects of imitation are "men in action." By action he means, besides physical actions, all manifestations of psychical energy, such as passions, emotions and character and everything that expresses the mental life that reveals a rational personality. The proper nature of an artwork can be grasped as a representation of energy, of passion, of thought and of "action," not as the static copy of a natural object. "Action" implies the dynamic notion of matter as energy in an ever-changing condition of space and time.

3. The Spirit-Matter Dialectic in the Art of the Middle Ages

The history of art has constantly experienced the tension of a dialectic relationship between the static and the dynamic understandings of art. In the Middle Ages the iconoclastic controversy over images was an occasion to clarify the proper meaning of a true image and to show how an "icon" (image) is different from an "idol." In the light of the biblical interdiction of idol-making and worship it is made clear that an idol is an object which has no meaning beyond itself.[2] It is condemned because it is "end in itself" and is not open to the world relationships. An idol is a product of human pride, greed and ignorance. As a self-contained object, it has no revelatory potential. It lacks dynamism and hence its effectiveness.

On the other hand, an icon is understood as a dynamic object. It is spatial and relational since it transcends its material definitions and opens itself to the revelation of the Spirit and spiritual realities. It undergoes a transfiguration of revelatory nature through a critical, creative process of "self-sacrifice" or "self-emptying." Thus, an icon becomes a term of revelation, making visible what is invisible. The

[2] The dynamic meaning of "image" is emphasized in the Old Testament by the interdiction of all man-made images which are but attempts to objectify God, restricting him to the limitations of human artefacts. "You shall not make yourselves a graven image or any likeness of anything that is in heaven above, or that is in the earth beneath, or that is in the water under the earth; you shall not bow down to them or serve them" (Ex 20:4-5). Idols are condemned because they are products of human ignorance and delusion (Is 41:29). Only God can be the author of his own image. Prophets would condemn idol worship as immorality (Jer 44.1-5) and breach of faith in God. It is nothing but pursuing "worthless things" of human fascination and greed (Jer 2:5).

spatial and relational nature of the icons is implied in the liturgical and communitarian character of icons. Icons stand for presence, communion and celebration.

4. Exploration of the "Outer Space" in the Renaissance Art

The Renaissance art marked a turning point in the history of European art, as it revived the values of humanism once flourished in the classical Greek culture and art. While the medieval art had a tendency to negate "this world" for the sake of the "other world," the Renaissance art attempted to explore and rediscover the good things of this world, the pleasures of the senses, the beauty and the bounty of Nature and the hidden knowledge of the phenomenal world.

The explorative and scientific mentality of the time is reflected also in the artistic experiments of the time. The beauty of the physical space fascinated the Renaissance artists and they tried to capture and represent it in their art and architecture. Artistic skill was demonstrated in the mastery of perspective, anatomy and design. Renaissance artists presupposed in their works the notion of a static space and time.

5. Romanticism and the Interest in the "Inner Space"

The age of Romanticism witnessed a critical phase in art. It opened art to a space of innumerable possibilities. Being an age of revolutions and violent emotional outbursts, the art of the Romantic age had to grapple with the psychological conflicts which were characteristic of the time. The emergence of physical sciences restricted the scope of art in exploring the outer, physical world. Consequently artists turned their attention to the inner, psychological world of feelings and emotions. They began to be concerned about themselves, being subjective in the choice of their themes and styles.

Art of modern times rebelled against the restrictive classical notions of art, as they explored the "inscape" of their own selves and depicted the fears, hopes, frustrations, loneliness, fantasies, perceptions, actions and dreams. Artists were concerned about their individual views and experiences. Modern art broke out in different directions as different movements and experiments. What is strikingly visible in modern art is the disintegration of image. The concept of image in art has lost its objectivity and concreteness. It has become fragmented, deformed, abstract and surreal. Since art was preoccupied with many important questions vital to life, beauty ceased to be a concern of art. The skill of the artist was considered to be predominantly intellectual than physical.

One of the important concerns of modern art is the search for the spiritual. It is evident in the works of Caspar David Friedrich and the Joseph M. Turner. They infused their landscape paintings with a sense of divinity. Before the Romantic period the sense of the sacred could be seen in the representational content of the works. But during and after the Romantic period artists faced with the problem expressing their spiritual experiences without traditional themes of Christian art. They turned to abstract art and tried to attain new dimensions of consciousness.

6. Abstraction and the Search for the Spiritual in Art

The artists of abstract art were influenced by different Western and Eastern traditions of mysticism. Wassily Kandinsky and Piet Mondrian are said to have been influenced by theosophy as they adopted abstraction in their paintings. They searched for secret soul of things. Mondrian searched for changeless pure reality behind the changing natural forms.[3]

Paul Klee in his abstract paintings gave the design of a possible world, revealing the fundamental idea behind the coincidental. For Klee, the making of art was a simile for the creation of the world. He was not interested in the formal products of nature, but in the formative forces. He attempted to capture nature in terms of primal images and discovered analogies to the universal design even in the tiniest leaf.[4]

For Franz Marc, the goal of art was to "reveal the unearthly life dwelling behind everything, to break the mirror of life so that we may look being in the face." Abstract expressionism has offered different possibilities of experimentation. American artist Jackson Pollock has given expression to uninhibited, spontaneous action in his "action paintings," while there are also artists who have experimented with objectless, non-figurative paintings evoking a meditative experience.

---

[3] See Aniela Jaffé, "Symbolism in the Visual Arts" in *Man and His Symbols*, ed. Carl Jung. London: Picador, 1978 (1964), 291.

[4] Karl Ruhrberg, "Painting" in *Art of the 20th Century*, Vol. 1, ed. Ingo F. Walther, Köln: Taschen, 2005, 112-13.

Artists like Mark Tobey, Barnett Newman, Mark Rothko and Ad Reinhardt proposed in their abstract artworks immediate experiences of space.

The works of Lucio Fontana with "holes" (*buchi*) and "slits" (*tagli*) are intended for the penetration of space into them. He punched holes in the canvas or slit it with a knife in order to violate matter to make room, to create space for the visualisation of an idea. He named these works as "spatial concepts" (*concetto spaziale*). Fontana paved the way to further experiments in spatial and environmental art forms.

7. Shift from Art Objects to Space and Environment

In contemporary art there are various other experiments which reflect the bewildering developments in the social, economic and cultural life we witness today. It is impossible to define art; we may try to identify it rather than define it. Among the various strains of artistic creativity in contemporary art we can observe an effort to redefine the understanding of image. It consists in an attempt to expand the scope of the art work by transcending its limitation of being an isolated object. An artwork in this sense is not an object but a configuration or a constellation, referring to a spatial experience.

The new trend in art which began in the 1960s was a reaction to excessive "subjectivism" found in Expressionist tendencies and their psychological interpretations. It also overcame the Constructivist views of composition. These artworks were endowed with kinetic energy and they were supposed to interact with the environment. According to Hans Haacke, "A sculpture that physically reacts to environment and/or affects its surroundings is no longer to be regarded as an object. The range of outside factors influencing it, as well as its own radius of action reach beyond the space it mathematically occupies."[5] The sculptural forms integrated nature, light, movement and technology into them. They could be oscillating, floating, dangling, rotating, vibrating, rising or sinking.

Among contemporary art forms, site-specific sculpture, land art, earth art, environmental art, installations, happenings, performances and

---

[5] See, Manfred Schneckenburger, "Sculpture" in *Art of the 20th Century*, Vol. 2, ed. Ingo F. Walther, Köln: Taschen, 2005, 500.

many other similar art forms have the experience of a dynamic space as their prominent theme. Most of the artworks which have space as their theme resist to be "commodified." They are known to the posterity through documentation. They give less attention to their objective or figurative qualities than to their effectiveness to re-create, re-interpret or change the space around them for their viewers.

Environmental artworks are open to interact with the viewers, making them active participants rather than passive admirers. They seek to diminish the distance between art and life and integrate artistic experience to the experiences of life. At the same time, they strike the eyes of the viewers through their exaggerated scales or proportions or through their settings and locations. The art forms like "Happenings" and "Performances" defy the objective, commodified nature of artworks by working with non-permanent, organic materials and giving greater importance to action and the space of action. They have the typical qualities of a ritual, and the artist play a priestly role in the performance, even though in a secular context.

In contemporary art we find a new development of the notion of artistic creativity which explores the dynamic nature of space. It means that artworks are not mere static, isolated objects to be valued for their physical qualities. They are references or witnesses to a spatial change and therefore themselves dynamic entities belonging to a web of relationships. Thus contemporary art proposes an art experience in terms of participation, communion and celebration.

If we take an overall view of the tendencies in art history we find a transition in the understanding of artistic creativity; it has become less object-oriented and more space-oriented. It has moved away from representation objects in static images. For some time it explored the secrets of the phenomenal world with the sharpness of a scientific mind. Then it turned inward to the inner world of the artist's experiences and to express the bewildering world of emotions, feelings and actions. Contemporary art emerges with the notion of a dynamic space of interrelatedness. Artistic creativity consists not in the production of isolated images but in creating works of spatial configurations with underlying webs of relationships. Active participation and involvement of the viewers in the work make it an event.

8. Dynamic "Space-Time" – Meeting Point of Mysticism and Science

Mystical awareness has to do with space and time awareness. In spite of their differences in giving stress to the different aspects of their experience, mystics all over the world and of all time agree in some fundamental characteristics. They all agree in the essentials of their basic word-view. One of the shared characteristics of all mystics is the awareness of the fundamental unity and the interrelatedness all things. They experience the phenomenal world as the manifestation of the One reality. Their vision penetrates through the apparent multiplicity of existence and their discerning mind perceives the interdependence of all things which ultimately constitutes a cosmic whole. *Visvam ekam* (all things are one) is thus a central characteristic mystic experience. In our practical life we do not have the awareness of the unity of all things; we find them as separate objects and deal with them accordingly. We have to struggle against our intellect to believe in the fundamental unity of reality and to accept that our concepts of separate things and events are products of our intellect. Mystics would consider it as illusion.

A breakthrough in our understanding of the world has occurred through the recent developments physics. According to Fritjof Capra, "The basic oneness of the universe is not only the central characteristic of the mystical experience, but is also one of the most important revelations of modern physics. [...] As we study various models of subatomic physics we shall see that they express again and again, in different ways, the same insight – that the constituents of matter and the basic phenomena involving them are interconnected, interrelated and interdependent; that they cannot be understood as isolated entities, but as integrated parts of the whole."[6]

In the late 1920s Niels Bohr and Werner Heisenberg put forward the quantum theory, the theory of atomic phenomena, which implies the essential interconnectedness of nature. This theory shows that "the subatomic particles are not isolated grains but are probability patterns, interconnections in an inseparable cosmic web that includes the human observer and her consciousness."[7]

---

[6] F. Capra, *The Tao of Physics*, New York: Bantam Books, 1984 (1976[1]), 117.

[7] F. Capra, *The Turning Point: Science, Society and Rising Culture*, London: Flamingo, 1982, 83.

Crucial to the new awareness of reality is also a new understanding of space and time. Classical physics was built upon the notion of an absolute, three-dimensional space, independent of the materials it contained. But the modern physics has revealed that the concepts of space and time are constructs of human mind; they do not belong to the nature of reality. This is in conformity with the experience of the mystics. According to Capra, "The Eastern mystics link the notions of both space and time to particular states of consciousness. Being able to go beyond the ordinary state through meditation, they have realized that the conventional notions of space and time are not the ultimate truth. The refined notions of space and time resulting from their mystical experiences appear to be in many ways similar to the notions of modern physics as exemplified by the theory of relativity."[8]

According to the relativity theory of Einstein all space and time measurements are relative; they have no absolute significance. They are only the elements of a language by which an observer describes his environment. Each observer can have his or her description of the natural phenomena. Such observations are subjective. Thus the classical concepts of an absolute space and time are abandoned.

The theory of relativity adds the concept of "time" to the three-dimensional space as a fourth dimension. Thus space and time are inseparably connected and form a four-dimensional continuum which is called "space-time."

The discoveries of the quantum theory and the relativity theory lead us to the understanding of a dynamic universe, which is at the same time a web of relationships. It is different from the previous scientific notion of the universe as a changeless three-dimensional space in the form of a container of isolated, independent objects. "The dynamic aspect of matter arises in quantum theory as a consequence of the wave-nature of subatomic particles, and is even more essential in relativity theory, [...] where the unification of space and time implies that the being of matter cannot be separated from its activity. The properties of subatomic particles can therefore only be understood in a dynamic context; in terms of movement, interaction and transformation."[9]

---

[8] F. Capra, *The Tao of Physics*, 150.

[9] F. Capra, *The Tao of Physics*, 178.

Awareness of a dynamic space-time with movement, flow, constant change and transformation is characteristic of mystic experiences. Mystics testify also to their experience of the unity and integrity of the universe constituted by a web of relationships, whose interconnections are dynamic, alive, moving and growing. Dr. Radhakrishnan writing about the Buddhist world-view says: "A wonderful philosophy of dynamism was formulated by Buddha 2,500 years ago. [...] Impressed with the transitoriness of objects, the ceaseless mutation and transformation of things, Buddha formulated a philosophy of change. He reduces substances, souls, monads, things to forces, movements, sequences and processes and adopts a dynamic conception of reality."[10] For mystics their experience of reality is necessarily connected with the awareness of a dynamic space of interrelatedness of everything. Such a space can be aptly described as a "creative space." It is a field of energy where creation and recreation take place.

9. Notion of a Dynamic "Space-Time" in Art

Creativity implies transforming relationships. Creative space is characterised by transformations which continually bring to existence a cosmos of relationships out of isolation, desolation, death and decay. It is from this understanding of creativity that we can come to consider the notion of space as vital to the understanding of artistic creativity. Art is supposed to mediate between the material and the spiritual realms by creating the awareness of a space which is characterised by transformation, participation and celebration.

The notion of a dynamic space-time is common to art as well as mysticism. The human need for art is not fulfilled only by producing objects which are useful and beautiful. Art explores subjective realms of experience and finds expression in creations of a dynamic nature. "The function of art is to redeem material objects from their static isolation by transferring them to the realm of dynamic relativity."[11]

---

[10] S. Radhakrishnan, *Indian Philosophy*, New York: Macmillan, 1958, 367.

[11] S. Elavathingal, "Ashram and a Spirituality of Creative Space" in *New Horizons of Indian Christian Living*, ed. Saju Chackalackal, Bengaluru: Vidyavanam Publications, 2009, 129.

An artwork suggests a field of energy in which there are no isolated objects, but configurations in a web of relationships. The trends in contemporary art only confirm the view of art in all traditional cultures, which is predominantly ritual and religious. In all traditional cultures religion and art are inseparably related to each other. The function of art in religion is to create a "dynamic space" for communitarian celebration. A religious ritual can be seen as a "*Gesamtkunstwerk*" incorporating different art forms appealing to all the senses and involving the whole human person. It transposes the participants into a new realm or space which is characterised by of a new awareness of relationships.

All religious art in the form of images, rituals and edifices have this dynamic spatial meaning as far as their effectiveness is concerned. An image in the Indian religious tradition, for example, is not a static object, but a "*mandala*" or a field of energy, which presupposes an ever-changing condition of space-time.[12] In the Byzantine tradition, an icon is differentiated from an idol because of its dynamic nature. "In order to become the *contemporary* of the believer contemplating it, the icon disengages itself from specific localities and from time,"[13] while an idol is known under conditions of fixed place and time. Due to its static nature its effectiveness is confined to itself. On the other hand, "in contemplating the icon, the beholder is meant to be led beyond the forms to the frontiers of the undepictable: not by the suppression or the disregard of forms, but by going beyond them, that is, by that long journey which does not arbitrarily violate the visual function by some intellectual trick but turns our beings from the visible to the invisible, by an authentically mystical path that leads us into the night of the senses."[14]

---

[12] See A. Coomaraswamy, *The Transformation of Nature in Art*, New York: Dover Publications, 1956 (1934[1]), 31. According to Coomaraswamy, a traditional artist depicts not a particular moment of time, an arrested action, but a continuous condition. As to what is meant by a continuous condition, the dance of Siva takes place not merely in Taraka forest, nor even at Chidambaram, but in the heart of the worshipper.

[13] G. Limouris, "The Microcosm and Macrocosm of the Icon: Theology, Spirituality and Worship in Colour" in *Icons – Windows on Eternity: Theology and Spirituality in Colour*, Geneva: WCC Publications, 1990, 108.

[14] G. Limouris, "The Microcosm and Macrocosm of the Icon: Theology, Spirituality and Worship in Colour," 108-109.

10. The "Loss of Space" and the "Regaining of Space"

In all traditional philosophies and religions the existence of the manifold world is attributed to the work of a Creator. In the Bible it is Yahweh who creates cosmos out of chaos by the power of his word.[15] The "Art" of divine creativity consists in creating a configuration of relationships rather than producing a world of many isolated objects as creatures. The world is, then, a vibrant and dynamic "field of interrelatedness" in which God is present, manifesting himself through his actions of power and wisdom.

The biblical stories of creation underscore not only the centrality of human beings in creation but also their relatedness to the rest of creation either as the apex of a pyramid (Gen 1) or as the centre of a circle (Gen 2).[16] This truth is implied in the statement that God created human beings in his own "image and likeness."[17] The expression "image and likeness" does not imply any static object or entity representing God, but the power and glory of God manifested in his creative act. "Image" in this context is a dynamic notion, which cannot be idolized. It speaks about an action of God, not about the nature of humanity.[18] It is the glory of God revealed in the unity, integrity and harmony of creation. But human disobedience disrupted the divine design and it needed to be re-created and restored.

In the story of Adam and Eve the loss of Paradise is the loss of "space." Paradise stands for an ideal space of relationships which is presided over by God's all-pervading presence. There is a fatal rupture in the companionship between God and the first human couple. Till that time Adam and Eve enjoyed the company of God and they lived happily with the rest of creation in the divine presence. It was pleasing to God to see his creation and to be with it (Gen 2:31).

---

[15] According to Meister Eckhart, "All creatures are words of God." See M. Fox, *Breakthrough: Meister Eckhart's Creation Spirituality in New Translation,* New York: Image Books, 1980, 58. According to Rg Veda III.38.1, the Divine Maker is Tvastr, a carpenter. In Rg Veda X.72.2 the Creator is a smith.

[16] See, Karl Hermann Schelkle, *Theology of the New Testament, vol. 1: Creation*, trans. William A. Jürgens, Collegeville, Minn: Liturgical Press, 1968, 83.

[17] *Genesis*, 1:26-27; 5:1; 9:6.

[18] See, Claus Westermann, Genesis *1-11, A Commentary*, trans. John J. Seullion, Minneapolis: Augsburg Publishing House, 1984, 155.

But after the "fall" everything turned upside down. Adam and Eve were ashamed of themselves to come to the presence of God. They tried to avoid God and hid themselves from the sight of God. God called to Adam, "Where are you?" and Adam responded from his hiding place (Gen 3:9-10). This shift in communication from seeing to hearing points to the existential "dislocation" of Adam and Eve, in relation to God and to the rest of the creation. They were distanced from the "centre" and became victims of conflict in the periphery, as they were banished from the garden. The fall of the first parents had a very tragic repercussion in their progeny. Cain murdered his own brother Abel! Sin is the loss of divine presence which darkens human mind and blinds human vision incapacitating a person even to recognize his own brother. It causes the destruction of the cosmic order and harmony and shreds the fabric of all relationships. God asked Cain, "Where is your brother Abel" (Gen 4:9)? By this question Cain was challenged in his conscience to see where he stood in relation to his brother. Cain responded, "I do not know."

Cain's ignorance had catastrophic effects on himself and on the environment. He had to bear the curse of the ground soaked by the blood of Abel. Cain was late to realize that as the aftermath of his fatal act he was being banished from God's sight and was condemned to be a wanderer on earth. Cain said, "Today you have driven me away from the soil, and I shall be hidden from your face; I shall be a fugitive and a wanderer on the earth" (Gen 4:13-14).

An existential "displacement" is thus deeply ingrained to human nature in relation to God and in relation to the fellow human beings. It is from the poignant awareness of a loss and separation that the pilgrimage of life and the search towards reunion begins. It progresses by mending the broken threads of relationships, retracing the footprints God to the paradise and regaining the lost space of communion, harmony and celebration.

In Christian theology the notion of "image and likeness" implies a task and an opportunity for creative engagement in the world. It is the well-spring of Christian imagination and creativity. Christian theology elaborates the notion of the "image of God" applying it to Jesus Christ who is the centre of the new creation. According to St. Paul: "He is the image of the invisible God, the firstborn of all creation; for in him all things in heaven and on earth were created, things visible and invisible [...]. All things have been created through him and for him. He himself is before all things and in him all things hold together" (Col 1:15-17). Jesus Christ is the unique mediator between the Creator and the creatures, supporting the universe and maintaining everything in harmony.

11. The "Dispersed Space" and its "Re-Integration"

While the biblical story describes the human condition in terms of a "fall" and alienation from divine grace, there are other world traditions which attempt to explain the existential tension which characterizes human life as a fracture or dispersal of the original cosmic unity and harmony. For example, in *Śatapatha Brāhmana* the Prajāpati myth tries to explain on the one hand the original and organic oneness of the universe and, on the other, its existential plurality.

In his creative fervour (*tapas*) the Lord of creatures (Prajāpati) dismembers himself and falls into pieces. The original unity is broken in the creative act. "Now the Lord of creatures, having brought forth living beings, felt himself as it were emptied. The creatures turned away from him; nor did they abide with him for his joy and for his sustenance."[19] Here the allusion is that the whole of creation came to existence as a result of the primordial self-sacrifice (*yajña*) of Prajāpati.

The Rgvedic hymn of *Purusa Sūkta*[20] while narrating how the creation of the universe took place, speaks of the immolation of the primordial Man and the dismembering of his limbs. The entire universe - animate and inanimate world, elements and cosmic forces – came into existence from the different parts of his body. In this hymn the emphasis on the universality and the spatial nature of the Purusa rather than on his human features.

Purusa himself is identified with the sacrifice through which he extends himself in the universe. He, as the sacrifice, represents the total space-time reality of the universe and all its domains. The root of the word *yajña* (sacrifice) is *yaj* which means originally the gesture of "offering,"

---

[19] *Śatapata Brahmana,* III. 9. 1.1.

[20] *Rg Veda,* X. 90.1-16

the act of "stretching out" and "extending."[21] The entire cosmos has a sacrificial nature, since it is a product of the primordial sacrifice. The world owes its origin and its continued existence to sacrifice.

12. Ritual Arts and the Re-Integration of the Cosmic Space

The various accounts of the origin of the cosmos, in spite their striking differences in many aspects, have something in common. First of all, they affirm an inner relatedness of all the creatures to the creator and among themselves. Secondly, they search into the sources of human creativity. In the Indian myths, the entire universe is organically related to its Creator. It implies that they have some meaning or "significance" even in their bewildering diversity of forms and in their apparent incomprehensibility. In other words, the entire creation has a "centre," or a "heart" which gives it sense and hold.

According to Rg Veda, "the notions of all created things are inherent in him who is as it were the hub within the wheel."[22] The relationship of the One to the many can be thus demonstrated by the symbol of the wheel. Consider the wheel as two concentric circles. Each point on the outer circle has a corresponding and analogous point on the inner one. Even when the inner circle is reduced to coincide in a unity, this relation is maintained. "In other words, all the radii, all individual principles and their total extension are represented at their common centre *in principio*, in an inconnumerable principle (*tattva*), which is at the same time an altogether simple substance (*dharma*), and possessed of a multifarious nature (*svabhava*); a single point, and yet for each radius its own and private starting point."[23]

The source of human creativity is the existential tension between the One and the many which has a creative nature. The myths of origin underscore the fact that the created world is a dynamic and vibrant

---

[21] See W. D. Whitney *The Roots, Verb Forms and Primary Derivatives of the Sanskrit Language*. Leipzig, 1885, 20ff. cited in L. Malieckal. *Yajña and Eucharist*, Bangalore: Dharmaram Publications, 1989, 26.

[22] *Rg Veda*, VIII.41.6.

[23] A. Coomaraswamy, "Vedic Exemplarism" in *Coomaraswamy: Selected Papers* Vol 2: *Metaphysics*, Bollingen Series LXXXIX, ed. Roger Lipsey. Princeton: Princeton University Press, 1977, 179.

reality, which evolves and progresses towards a goal or a peak point.[24] This historical process is directed to an ultimate Communion. Implied is that it is a creative task that is to be accomplished in history. This task is entrusted to the creative power and agency of the humans, who are to work as artists to fulfil the task of reconstructing the universe. The existential inversion and dispersal of the world has thus become a chance, an opportunity for human creativity.

In the language of the myths the reconstruction of the universe, the "re-membering" of the cosmic body, is also a *yajña* (sacrifice). *Śatapatha Brāhmana* VI.1.2.12-13 reads: When he had procreated all beings and run through the whole gamut of creation he fell into pieces [...]. When he was fallen into pieces his breath departed from the midst of him, and when his breath had departed, the Gods abandoned him. He said to Agni, "Put me, I pray to you, together again."[25] Thus Vedic sacrifice has a creative and re-creative meaning. Its complete trajectory begins from heaven, passes through the earth and culminates again in heaven.

In the biblical vision the existential inversion through the original sin is rectified in the resurrected body of Christ who suffered and died a sacrificial death. In his letter to the Ephesians (1:15-22) St. Paul speaks of the restoration of the universe in the body of Christ.

---

[24] Ken Wilber describes this process in terms of an involution-evolution process referring to different thinkers who have attempted to explain the cosmic process in evolutionary terms. For example, the great German idealist Schelling is said to have maintained that history is an epic with two parts; the first part depicts the departure of humanity from its centre, namely, the Spirit up to its furthest point of alienation and the second part depicts the return. The first is the Iliad and the second the Odyssey of history. The first movement is centrifugal, that is, outward, dispersive, separative, kenotic, dismembering and the second movement is centripetal, that is, inward, re-collective, re-unifying and re-membering. See, Ken Wilber, *Up From Eden: A Transpersonal View of Human Evolution*, Boston: New Science Library, 1986, 309. Similarly, Aurobindo holds that Brahman gets lost in involution and then evolves back from matter to *prana* to mind to over-mind to super-mind and Atman. This is a cosmological as well as a psychological process. See, Ken Wilber, *Up From Eden: A Transpersonal View of Human Evolution*, Boston: New Science Library, 1986, 313.

[25] Again in *Taittiriya Brāhmana* II, 3,6,1: When he had produced the creatures, Prajāpati fell into pieces. Being reduced to a (mere) heart he was lying exhausted. He uttered a cry: 'Alas, my life!' The waters heard him. They came to his aid and by means of sacrifice of the Firstborn they restored to him his sovereignty.

sacrificial death. In his letter to the Ephesians (1:15-22) St. Paul speaks of the restoration of the universe in the body of Christ.

13. Art and the "Blissful Space"

The task of art is the reconstruction of the universe. It is a process of the rediscovery of the "lost space." The nostalgic yearning for a harmonious, blissful space of communion and celebration is deeply rooted in human consciousness. It is expressed in art forms, in which space is an important theme. The "circle" or "sphere" is one of the most recurring motifs appearing in the art of all ages and peoples. It is a very enduring and significant expression of human self-consciousness. It expresses the totality of the human psyche in all aspects, including the relationship between human beings and to the whole of nature. The most vital aspect of life which the circle symbolism expresses is the ultimate wholeness of life.[26]

In traditional cultures all arts, especially ritual arts, are performed in view of attaining the wholeness of life which depends on one's alignment to the cosmic process. Cosmos is viewed as a continuum.[27] Like a circle the universal order has an uninterrupted continuity of space and time. There is no break anywhere in the chain of existential forms, including human beings. Moreover, each link in the chain is a miniature of the whole.

Consequently, in the consciousness of every human being there is an inner space of immanence (*Ātman*) corresponding to the outer space of transcendence (*Brahman*). Contemplative self-awareness "in-tends" (tends inward) and, at the same time, "ex-tends" (tends outward) to a cosmic awareness. According to the five-fold layer (*pañcakośa*) theory of consciousness,[28] the *annamaya kosa* (the food layer) is the outermost level of consciousness and the *ānandamaya kosa* (the bliss layer) is the innermost core of consciousness. The bliss-consciousness is the state in which one attains pure awareness, transcending the subject-object

---

[26] See, Aniela Jaffé, "Symbolism in the Visual Arts" in *Man and His Symbols*, ed. Carl Jung, London: Picador, 1978 (1964), 266.

[27] See Ajit Mukherjee, *Ritual Art in India*, London: Thames & Hudson, 1985, 153.

[28] *Taittiriya Upanisad*, III.1.1-III.6.1.

duality. It is the experience of *rasa,* the highest enjoyment, which said to be the nature of the divine Self (*Brahman*).

Divine creativity is the overflow of the divine bliss which accounts for the spontaneity and efficiency of the Creator. In other words, the creative act is an expression of the Creator's own being. The cosmic order, rhythm, harmony and beauty reflect the blissful nature of divine creativity which makes creation a play (*līlā*). Human creativity, as manifested in various spatial art forms, is an effort to attain the bliss-consciousness. In the case of ritual arts, the consecration of the sacred space is an "imitation" of the original and ideal space of order, rhythm, harmony and the blissful divine-human communion. The construction of sanctuaries and altars is considered as the reconstruction of the world and they are believed to be situated at the "centre of the universe."[29]

Mandala in the Indian and the cross-form in the Christian tradition of art and architecture are spatial concepts of harmony and union of all opposites, such as, the One and the many, inside and outside, above and below, heaven and earth. They are "locations" of creation and re-creation where God and the artist meet. As Meister Eckhart would say, it is where God's goodness, his word "flows out" in creation but returns and "remains within."[30]

14. Conclusion

Mysticism is basically a search for Unity in the world of diversity and multiplicity. It implies a dialectical relationship between the physical world of the "many" and the metaphysical world of the "One." All religions and spiritual traditions have developed their theologies and practices as paths to mysticism. Broadly speaking, there can be two different approaches to mysticism: an "essential" approach and an "existential" approach. The former seeks to answer questions like "who is God?" and "who am I?" while the latter engages itself with questions such as "where is God?" and "where am I?"

---

[29] Mircea Eliade, Patterns in Comparative Religion, London: Sheed & Ward, 1958, 371.

[30] M. Fox, *Breakthrough: Meister Eckhart's Creation Spirituality in New Translation,* New York: Image Books, 1980, 65.

The inquiry into the nature of God cannot proceed in positive terms and hence it is forced to depend on abstract concepts. On the other hand, the questions of the "whereabouts" of God and oneself on relational terms are disposed to trace a path through concrete realities, developing a positive theology of creative nature, because it begins from the awareness and affirmation of the world. The world as the venue of divine revelation and human realization is to be understood as a "dynamic space" of divine and human creativity. The "original" creative notion of space is not that of a static three-dimensional space which functions as a container of things. It is a four dimensional "space-time," a condition of continuous change which makes it a field of energy. The "Art" of God consists in creating a configuration of relationships rather than producing a world of many isolated objects as creatures. The world is, then, a vibrant and dynamic field of interrelatedness in which God is present, manifesting himself through his actions of power and wisdom.

For human beings, who are "fallen" and existentially disintegrated, the path of realization is to reconstruct and re-create the universe. The religious ritual arts of all traditional cultures envisage a re-integration into the wholeness and fullness of life. The secularized art of the 19th and 20th centuries, even though freed itself from the influence of religion, struggled to discover the "spiritual" in art as the experience of a "space" within the subject. Contemporary art has come out of the subjective and psychological realm to discover spiritual dynamism of the "space" outside by creating works which suggest action, communion and participation. Artistic experience has become "elemental" and environmental. Both in art and mysticism "transcendence" consists in the experience of "space" as communion and re-integration. The artistic and the mystical consciousness is extension to a space of interrelatedness of all beings. An art work, in this sense, is experienced and judged as "spatial."

References

01. Capra, F., *The Tao of Physics*, New York: Bantam Books, 1984.

02. Capra, F., *The Turning Point: Science, Society and Rising Culture*, London: Flamingo, 1982.

03. Coomaraswamy, A., *The Transformation of Nature in Art*, New York: Dover Publications, 1956.

04. Elavathingal, S., "Ashram and a Spirituality of Creative Space" in *New Horizons of Indian Christian Living*, ed. Saju Chackalackal, Bengaluru: Vidyavanam Publications, 2009, 127-132.
05. Eliade, M., *Patterns in Comparative Religion*, London: Sheed & Ward, 1958.
06. Fox, M., *Breakthrough: Meister Eckhart's Creation Spirituality in New Translation*, New York: Image Books, 1980.
07. Jaffé Aniela, "Symbolism in the Visual Arts" in *Man and His Symbols*, ed. Carl Jung, London: Picador, 1978 (1964[1]), 266.
08. Jung, C., ed. *Man and His Symbols*, London: Picador, 1978 (1964[1]).
09. Limouris, Gennadios, "The Microcosm and Macrocosm of the Icon: Theology, Spirituality and Worship in Colour" in *Icons – Windows on Eternity: Theology and Spirituality in Colour*, Geneva: WCC Publications, 1990.
10. Lipsey, R., *Coomaraswamy: Selected Papers* Vol 2: *Metaphysics*, Bollingen Series LXXXIX, Princeton: Princeton University Press, 1977.
11. Malieckal, L., Yajña *and Eucharist,* Bangalore: Dharmaram Publications, 1989.
12. Mukherjee, Ajit, *Ritual Art in India*, London: Thames & Hudson, 1985.
13. Radhakrisnan, S., *Indian Philosophy*, New York: Macmillan, 1958.
14. Ruhrberg, Carl, "Painting" in *Art of the 20th Century*, vol. 1, ed. Ingo F. Walther, Köln: Taschen, 2005.
15. Schelkle, K. H., Theology *of the New Testament, vol. 1: Creation*, trans. William A. Jürgens, Collegeville, Minn: Liturgical Press, 1968.
16. Walther, I. F., ed. *Art of the 20th Century*, Vols. 1 & 2, Köln: Taschen, 2005.
17. Westermann, C., *Genesis 1-11, A Commentary*, trans. John J. Seullion, Minneapolis: Augsburg Publishing House, 1984.
18. Whitney, W. D., *The Roots, Verb Forms and Primary Derivatives of the Sanskrit Language*, Leipzig, 1885.
19. Wilber, K., *Up From Eden: A Transpersonal View of Human Evolution*, Boston: New Science Library, 1986.

11

Mysticism and Art

Beyond Abstraction and Empathy

Dr. Stéphane Symons
Institute of Philosophy, K.U. Leuven, Belgium

Let me first start with a caveat: this article will not really address the topic of mysticism. It will not try to define what the mystic experience consists of and what sets it apart from, e.g. an "ordinary" religious or spiritual experience or, as the title of the article suggests, from an aesthetic experience. Instead, it will start with the description of what it is *not*: the mystic experience is *not*, I will contend, an experience in which a profound connection with the outside world is felt: it is *not* an experience of the absolute in which the borders between ego and *aliud* blur and Self and otherness are absorbed with one another. In this article, however, I *will* address the nature of the aesthetic experience, or more precisely, one specific type of aesthetic experience; i.e. the one that does away with any notion of absorption or reconciliation between the ego and the outside object. The article can in my opinion only be called successful if it manages to explain three things. The first thing it needs to explain is what the very recently deceased painter and musician Captain Beefheart might have meant when he was standing outside on the curb in front of the magnificent Vincent Van Gogh museum in Amsterdam and stated that he was "disappointed in the sun."

The second element that is important to the lecture is the following paragraph from Robert Walser's brilliant novel "The Tanners": "How charming women are whom you're allowed to race past without attracting their notice. How could you expect them to notice you? […] It's enough to have observant eyes yourself. […] The eyes of women on a morning street like this are so utterly splendid when they gaze off into the distance. Eyes looking past you are more beautiful then eyes that gaze directly at you. It's as if they lost something."[1]

The third task I have set myself is to explain why I was so utterly stunned, a couple of years ago, by the final scene of a dance performance titled *Keeping Still Part One*. This piece was both arranged and performed by Belgian choreographer and dancer Anne Theresa de Keersmaecker and was accompanied by both a recording of Gustav Mahler's *Lied von der Erde* and a remarkable sculpture made of light designed by Belgian visual artist Ann Veronica Janssens. At the end of the performance, when all dancing, music and lighting had stopped, a part of the back wall that separated the theatre stage from the world outside was pushed aside, granting the audience a direct view of a single tree, lit by a yellow spotlight and unaccompanied by anything but the sound of the wind rustling through its leaves.

Dictionaries usually define the term mysticism along the following lines: a heartfelt longing for a special union of the soul with God and of God with a human being. I will try to criticize this definition on all three grounds: i.e. the mystic experience is in my opinion *not* at all felt in the heart, it denotes the very *absence* of human longing and its *telos* is *not* a supposed "union" with God or with the universe. Allow me to go ahead and spoil the fun of this exercise by giving you its conclusions upfront: any experience that might come close to being called mystic can, in my view, only be a *physical* one pure and proper, involving the *entirety* of our bodies and not just our mental or emotional faculties. And instead of with a longing of a subject towards something exterior, or rather with a longing of a subject to bridge the gap with something exterior (the paradoxical longing to overcome longing), a mystical experience has in my mind to do with a responsiveness of a subject to the outside world *as* exterior and other; not with a *unio mystica*, that is to say, but with a form of desire that presupposes and acknowledges the fundamental distance that separates a subject from its desired object.

---

[1] Robert Walser, *The Tanners*, New York: New Directions, 2009, 218.

One way to criticize the concept of a *unio mystica* is through the concept of empathy, in German *Einfühlung*. In his influential book *Abstraction and Empathy* the German philosopher of art, Wilhelm Worringer, starts from the idea that artistic creation is motivated by what he, after the example of Alois Riegl, calls artistic volition and that this artistic volition, for its part, needs to be regarded as a quality of a "disputation of man with nature", a metaphysical "feeling about the world" or "a psychic state in which, at any given time, mankind found itself in relation to the cosmos."[2] Empathy, now, denotes a specific type of artistic volition, i.e. a very vitalistic and optimistic one, in which human beings are sufficiently comfortable with their surroundings to project their own vitality and energy into exterior objects. In this way, and this seems to be what marks empathy as a quality of the mystic experience, it denotes a profound connection between human beings and the outside world as the former are capable of enjoying themselves in and through the latter. "The precondition for the urge to empathy," writes Worringer, "is a happy pantheistic relationship of confidence between man and the phenomena of the external world"[3] and, in another formula, "Aesthetic enjoyment is objectified self-enjoyment: What I empathize into a sensuous object is quite generally life. And life is energy, inner working, striving and accomplishing. In a word, life is activity."[4]

Worringer opposes the need for empathy to the need for abstraction, which is a symptom of the inability to establish a profound contact with one's immediate environment and the escapist longing for a realm that does not refer to our surroundings. In empathy, on the contrary, the vector moves from a subject toward an object, most often an organic or natural one, to animate or enliven it, so that is recognized both as distinct from the Self and as nevertheless resonating with energetic qualities that we recognize as our own. Empathy is thus, as Freud will understand later on, a form of projection or annexation of the object and it presupposes, first, that the exteriority of the object is not experienced as inherently different from our selves and second, that this object which

[2] Wilhelm Worringer, *Abstraction and Empathy: A Contribution to the Psychology of Style*, Chicago: Ivan R. Dee, 2007, 12.

[3] Wilhelm Worringer, *Abstraction and Empathy*, 5.

[4] Wilhelm Worringer, *Abstraction and Empathy*, 5.

is not experienced as inherently different from ourselves is identical to itself, i.e. that it is, as Samuel Weber describes it, a "well-defined, self-contained place *into* which we can *feel* and project ourselves, or unload our feelings."[5] (Cf. also Worringer: "In empathizing this will to activity into another object, we are in the other object. We are delivered from our individual being as long as we are absorbed into an external object, an external form, with our inner urge to experience."[6]).

This sheds light on why the concept of empathy is an intimate companion to the concept of identification and why they have both an aesthetic and an ontological meaning, supporting not only Aristotle's philosophy of tragedy but also his metaphysics: it is only by clinging to a metaphysical belief in self-identical, unchanging and stabile forms and essences in things that one can maintain the possibility to have experiences, e.g. aesthetic ones, that overcome the contingency of what is inessential (matter, or the flux and arbitrariness of ordinary life) and "feel into" or profoundly know what is truly essential. No empathy, hence, without prior identification: no projection of one's own vitality onto an outside object without an experience of that outside object as complete and fully-present-to-itself. In a similar way, when twentieth century schools of acting that follow the Aristotelian tradition, e.g. the Lee Strasberg school of method acting believe in the ability of an actor to fully become one/empathize with his or her persona they inevitably presuppose the existence of fixed and stabile identities or character traits that those actors must first know/feel/identify in order to then identify *with*. Also for Benjamin, the concept of empathy brings art into the realm of metaphysics or religion and, by introducing the concept of aura, he, as well, denotes the possibility to enter into, unify, connect. "A person who concentrates [*sich Sammelnde*: collects himself] before a work of art is absorbed by it [*versenckt sich darein, geht in dieses Werk ein*]; he enters into the work, just as, according to legend, a Chinese painter entered his completed painting while beholding it."[7]

---

[5] Samuel Weber, "Citability- Of Gesture," Benjamin's –abilities, Cambridge and London: Harvard University Press, 2008, 106.

[6] Wilhelm Worringer, *Abstraction and Empathy*, 24.

[7] Walter Benjamin, "The Work of Art in the Age of Its Technological Reproducibility, Third Version," *Selected Writings*, Volume 4, 1938-1940, Howard Eiland and Michael

Benjamin's definition of the aura is the best possible way to think about quasi-mystical experiences of unity between subject and object: "Experience of the aura [...] arises from the fact that a response characteristic of human relationships is transposed to the relationship between humans and inanimate or natural objects. The person we look at, or who feels he is being looked at, looks at us in turn. To experience the aura of an object we look at means to invest it with the ability to look back at us."[8] What is at stake here is the possibility that outside things are in some sense endowed with a power of evocation and the idea that, in order to have this power of evocation, such objects need to some extent be spiritualized and recognized as familiar to the Self. When objects evoke something they "look back at us" with eyes not unlike our own, they become somewhat alive, despite their obvious objecthood and they become somehow unified and essentialized, despite their obvious arbitrariness or contingency. The idea that the power to express or evoke presupposes a self-identity or unity on the part of the object is still very often clung to, e.g. when it is thought that a variety of different sounds can only be recognized as music *despite* their obvious multiplicity (i.e. when multiple tones have become a tune), that words evoke meanings *despite* the arbitrariness of their physical presence (their sounds or outlook on the printed page) or that a painting evokes an image *despite* the obvious materiality of the paint (the materiality would be a mere analogon of the image, in Sartre's sense of the word).

Moreover, even in modernist thinking, that seems to have done away with the cult of genial creativity, embracing the very materiality and differentiated nature of the artwork, one can still encounter mystical ideas about the unity of the artwork and the profound feeling of connection it supposedly brings about between a human being and an outside object. Clement Greenberg's ideas about the "flash of the now" and the sublime experience we are meant to have in front of Mark Rothko's canvases presuppose that a work of art is encountered as a unity that has dispensed with all elements (sculpture-like illusion or symbolic content

W. Jennings, Cambridge and London: The Belknap Press of Harvard University Press, 2003, 268.

[8] Walter Benjamin, "On Some Motifs in Baudelaire," *Selected Writings*, Volume 4, 1938-1940, Howard Eiland and Michael W. Jennings, Cambridge and London: The Belknap Press of Harvard University Press, 2003, 338.

in the first place) that could distract our disembodied "eye that wanders through space." These ideas confuse aesthetic and religious notions on account of a presupposition that underlies philosophical thinking of art from that of Aristotle until that of Hume and that of Greenberg, i.e. the concept of an "autonomy of art", i.e. the idea that an object is an artwork on account of certain qualities that allow it to inherently differ from the ordinary objects we encounter in daily life. Artworks, hence, are supposed to have a different status and different characteristics than arbitrary objects: in them, to use Aristotle's vocabulary, matter gives way to form and, in successful theatre for instance, the unity of a coherent plot has replaced the multiplicity and flux of becoming of reality, thus allowing non-material and self-identical truths to be revealed. Or, using Hume's vocabulary from his essay on tragedy, it is on account of certain qualities that the artistic performance does not share with ordinary events, i.e. eloquence, the force of imagination, energy of expression and charms imitation that it triggers a combination of pleasure and horror that we cannot experience in real life.

Working my way up toward the three aims I have set myself at the beginning of this article, I will start with the last one I mentioned, i.e. to understand why it was moving, in the final act of the dance performance by Anne Theresa de Keersmaker, to see the back wall of the stage suddenly lifted and have a simple tree exposed to the eyes of the audience. To do this, I have to take an important step, rather limited in historical time but a major one in philosophical terms, i.e. the step from Hume to Kant. For the tree that was shown to the audience by De Keersmaker was in no way distinguished from an ordinary tree standing outside of the theatre; in fact, it *was* an ordinary tree standing outside of the theatre (behind the stage), yet it did bring about an aesthetic effect that I will not forget any time soon. In no way, hence, did this experience comply with Aristotle's, Hume's or, for that matter, Greenberg's claims that objects trigger aesthetic experiences on account of qualities that make them inherently different from arbitrary objects. In no way did the tree overcome or conceal its arbitrary nature when it brought about an aesthetic experience, thus proving that such experiences are not deductable from the objects that cause them and, moreover, that these experiences can, in fact, be caused by *any* object, a natural one just as well as an artwork.

In other words, the doctrine of the autonomy of the artwork was delivered a final blow, philosophically speaking, when Kant explored the *subjective* conditions of existence of the aesthetic experience and, artistically speaking, when Duchamp dragged a urinal into the gallery space and solemnly proclaimed it to be worthy of our aesthetic attention. With these two founding acts the era of the heteronomy of artworks saw the light of day: from then on everything could be called a work of art and the banal or trivial nature of an object did not any longer necessarily preclude the experience it brings about from being an aesthetic one. However, and this crucial point is all too often being forgotten, the end of the autonomy of art*works* does not at all entail the end of the autonomy of the aesthetic *experience*, quite the contrary. For the aesthetic *experiences* themselves that are caused by arbitrary objects do, however heteronomous and non-artistic these objects may be, inherently differ from our common experiences of these same objects: however ordinary the tree that was shown to us in the performance may have been, the experience that it gave rise to and that moved me so much certainly was not. Its moving and aesthetic effect, that is to say, was not due to the tree itself but to the sudden, surprising and unanticipatable experience of seeing it on stage. When looking at a simple tree in the midst of a dance-performance, our perception is essentially different from our normal, daily experience of that same tree. The tree, in other words, had remained the same; it was our set of eyes that had changed. Jacques Rancière has famously termed this complex combination of the heteronomy of artworks with the autonomy of the aesthetic experience the aesthetic regime and opposed it to what he calls the representational regime that dated back from Aristotle and lasted all the way until the end of the 18th century.

From the 19th century onwards, in the aesthetic regime, art has always included an element of non-art that it cannot any longer be separated from and has thus for once and for all destroyed its own earlier claims to bring about a more profound representation of truth or an expression of meaning. In the aesthetic regime, art does not any longer take a step back from reality in order to better understand it, by purifying the outside world from matter and locking up the flux of becoming in a coherent narrative but it fully embraces the outside world in an attempt to learn how to better respond to it. It is in a similar vein, in the context of a discussion of 19th and 20th century French composers, that Vladimir Jankélévitch talked about the "espressivo inexpressive", i.e. the specific (autonomous) aesthetic experience that issues forth from the (heteronomous) artistic attempt to render a direct voice to sounds from the outside world. Rather than aiming for an expression of a feeling (Romanticism) or for a depiction of the way in which certain phenomena are perceived by a listening subject (Impressionism), certain composers make themselves absent in order to reach the things themselves, i.e. "these things, these mute people, which speak a formless language that ignores intonation and the prosody of singing."[9] In his famous pieces inspired by bird-songs, Olivier Messiaen e.g. can neither be said to have adequately expressed bird-song, nor did he use bird-song to musically express a certain feeling, e.g. liberty, but he has managed to capture the sounds themselves, putting them to music in the most immediate way possible. "Only at the moment when one reaches things in themselves," Jankélévitch writes, "nature's voice itself, truth itself, only then does inexpressive music become expressive again. On the verge of losing its actual musical character, extreme realism becomes music again."[10]

However, this emphasis on the heteronomous nature of the artwork does not even touch upon the question what the autonomy of the aesthetic experience might consist of. If the aesthetic experience is, contrary to what Aristotle thought, not a way to distance oneself from reality in order to express or reveal what is essential to it, i.e. if it entails nothing less than a novel way of confronting that reality and of learning how to respond to it, what is it exactly about reality that we cannot allow ourselves to forget and what is it that we need to learn to cope with? The answer to this question is, in my opinion, at least as old as Pliny the Elder's famous story about the origin of art: for the reason why a lover bothers to trace the shadow cast by the head of his beloved one on a wall is that this simple, hastily sketched line allows him to deal with a feature of life that, however fundamental it may be, was all too

[9] Vladimir Jankélévitch, *La Musique et l'ineffable*, Paris: Éditions du Seuil, 1983, 51.
[10] Vladimir Jankélévitch, *La Musique et l'ineffable*, 53.

easily dismissed by Aristotle, Hume or Greenberg: change. Works of art become expressive or evocative when they confront the rhythm of life head on and do not at all distance themselves from reality in an attempt to reduce it to stabile forms. Art does not repress the outside world but merely, quite literally, frames it in a quest to embrace the movement of differentiation, becoming and change that mark it.

This view is diametrically opposed to the idea that expressive powers in objects presuppose a coherence or a unity and that, through this unity a profound connection with the Self is experienced. Instead, the combination of a heteronomous artwork with an autonomous aesthetic experience has discovered art as a means to react to the very becoming, flux, materiality and exteriority of the outside world. In this way, art becomes a "method", a way, a tao to learn how to respond to precisely these things that, to quote Aristotle's formula from book seven of the Poetics, "the eye can*not* take in all in at once" and to these phenomena that cannot ever, to repeat Greenberg's phrase, be grasped in a "flash of the now". Sounds, that is to say, do not become music *despite of* but *on account of* their multiplicity and temporal change or, more accurately put, by *way* of this multiplicity and temporal change, just like words express meaning *through* their arbitrariness and physical presence and paintings evoke images *through* the obvious materiality of the paint. It is here that the short passage written by Robert Walser that I quoted at the beginning of the article comes in. Walser describes there how, sometimes, a set of eyes can speak to us, not *despite of* the fact that they "look past us" but precisely *through* their indifference vis-à-vis our own gaze. Such eyes, looking past us, are the complete opposite of Benjamin's auratic eyes that "return our gaze" and thus set up an intimately felt connection between an exterior object and ourselves. The eyes described by Walser seem to "have lost something": they are always already on their *way* again, even in the very moment they cross our own eyes for a split second. They are not self-identical but constantly changing and becoming-other and it is their fleetingness which increases their power of expression and evocation. They, to borrow Samuel Weber's formula, *impart* because they ceaselessly *part with themselves*.

When artworks shed their autonomous status and become screens on which the very flux of life can ex-press itself, i.e. surfaces on which change and becoming leave behind incomplete traces or imprints, they do not give rise to a feeling, in the ego, that it recognizes itself in an outside object. All sense of empathy goes lost and the movement in which the Self can project its own life onto an exterior object, feeling into it, is replaced by a confrontation with an irreducible indifference of the object vis-à-vis the human being that looks at it. The vector, hence, has changed direction and, rather than going from subject to object, it goes from object to subject: it is the object which somehow becomes other, is released from its own identity and thus e-vokes something new, rather than that it would be the ego which projects and annexes the object, reducing it to what was already a part of that ego in the first place.

Walter Benjamin has coined a term that matches this experience in which the ego neither feels into/connects with an outside object nor falls victim to the escapist longing to suspend all ties with the outside world altogether. This term thus denotes a middle road between empathy and abstraction: *Zerstreeung*, both in the meaning of distraction and dispersal (being diffused or scattered). *Zerstreeung* is the opposite of *Sammlung* or absorption and refers to the reception of non-auratic, oftentimes mechanically made artworks, which cannot be annexed by the Self because, like film or photography (and music), they ceaselessly reveal elements that are utterly new and unanticipated by our consciousness. Artworks that are ceaselessly in motion and have time as an inherent element of their structure can neither be properly identified nor identified *with* and remain unstable and changing from beginning till end. "Reception in distraction," Benjamin wrote in by now very famous words, "[is] the sort of reception which is increasingly noticeable in all areas of art and is a symptom of profound changes of apperception. [It] finds in film its true training ground. Film, by virtue of its shock effects, is predisposed to this form of reception […]. The audience is an examiner, but a distracted one."[11]

Distraction is the middle ground between empathy and abstraction because it denotes a mental state in which our consciousness does not empathically recognize itself into the outside world yet does not

[11] Walter Benjamin, "The Work of Art in the Age of Its Technological Reproducibility. Third Version," 269.

withdraw into an abstract realm that has suspended all ties to that outside world: it manages to preserve our energetic investment in the world and life that surround us but precisely to the extent that that world and life are met as self-differentiating processes of becoming. Distraction is therefore not at all the opposite of attentiveness: on the contrary, it turns us into "examiners" of that which is not quite what it seems, that which is always taking leave of whatever meaning we had initially invested it with. There is nothing evocative about recognition per se and it is only in this sense that art-works can be said to be expressive, i.e. when they create something new, something that was not hitherto present, when they neither imitate nor re-present. Artworks do not create the illusion that something becomes present which in reality is not (Darstellen) but they reveal that side of reality that ceaselessly surprises because it cannot be reduced to what we had projected onto it. For this reason the old opposition between the supposed vagueness or abstract nature of art or depiction and the supposed concreteness or minuteness of reality or experience needs to be overthrown for once and for all: it is in art that we sharpen our attentiveness to such an extent that the clichés and presuppositions, the trivialities and common knowledge of our daily perceptions are shattered and that we learn how to look at reality afresh.

At least two things are interesting about this notion of distraction or *Zerstreeung*: the first one is that it is a distinctly *physical* form of apperception and the second one is that it is a distinctly *modern* one. The heightened awareness that reception in distraction grants us in order to allow us to perceive reality as something in flux is, in Benjamin's opinion, inseparably connected with a concept that is only included in the first three versions of his artwork-essay and was left out in the third, canonic one: the process of *innervation*. "*Die ungeheure technische Apparatur unserer Zeit zum Gegenstande der menschlichen Innervation zu machen*," writes Benjamin there, "*das ist die geschichtliche Aufgabe, in deren Dienst der Film seinen wahren Sinn hat*."[12] Innervation is the term for a directly physical reaction to reality that has bypassed the

[12] Walter Benjamin, "Das Kunstwerk im Zeitalter seiner technischen Reproduzierbarkeit. Erste Fassung," *Gesammelte Schriften*, Band I-2, Rolf Tiedemann and Herman Schweppenhäuser, Frankfurt am Main: Suhrkamp Verlag, 1991, 445.

mediation of our conscious minds and turns our bodies into quasi-hysterical surfaces that respond to *all* excitation and stimuli, regardless of whether they are important to our organism or not. Benjamin most likely picked up the term *Innervation* from Freud and Breuer's text on hysteria which describes it, in 1894, as a phenomenon of conversion, i.e. of transformation of unbearable and incompatible psychic excitation into "something somatic".[13] Innervation thus has a close connection with trauma since, in it, "excitation is forced into a wrong channel" which then becomes a "mnemic symbol" that remains alien and other-to-itself and is lodged "in consciousness like a sort of parasite."[14] It is for this reason that art becomes a "training ground"[15], as Benjamin puts it, when it induces an experience in which the aura is destroyed and our empathic response is circumvented: art has an edge to it that ordinary, domesticated life has not. If art e-vokes by doing away with our anticipation, if it ex-presses to the extent that it creates the new, it bypasses our pre-conceived differentiation between what is meaningful and what is not and, instead, learns us how to intuitively react to the slightest of all changes and shocks. Art trains us by increasing that type of human attentiveness that Freud, in his essay *Beyond the Pleasure Principle*, retraces to Angst, i.e. to a sense of impending danger, the source of which is most often unknown to the ego. Such attentiveness is, as Freud puts it, localized at the outer limits of our ego's and remains turned toward the outside world *as* exterior. Rather than the "most universal characteristic of our psychic processes" it needs to be called a "specific function of them": it protects (Abwehr) us from those things that come from outside and it teaches us how to cope with what can otherwise be harmful. *Zerstreuung*, innervation and attentiveness involve the entirety of our bodies (non-Merleau Ponty-like bodies since they do not presuppose an organic unity with the outside world), and

[13] Sigmund Freud, "The Neuro-Psychoses of Defence (I)," The Standard Edition of the Complete Psychological Works of Sigmund Freud, Volume 3, James Strachey, London: Hogarth, 1953-1974, 49. For an extensive analysis of this phenomenon of innervation see Miriam Bratu Hansen, "Benjamin and Cinema: Not a One-Way Street," *Critical Inquiry* 25. 2 ("Angelus Novus": Perspectives on Walter Benjamin, 1999): 315-320.
[14] Sigmund Freud, "The Neuro-Psychoses of Defence (I)," 49-50.
[15] Walter Benjamin, "The Work of Art in the Age of Its Technological Reproducibility," 269.

they denote artworks as phenomena that inevitably catch us offhand. Films and photographs, as we all know, are not created but *shot* and "the Dadaists turned the artwork into a missile. It jolted the viewer, taking on a tactile quality."[16]

For this reason, distraction is also a distinctly *modern* phenomenon. Not because, as Adorno would think, mass-entertainment and the culture industry have unconsciously put our minds to sleep but for precisely the opposite reasons. A modern universe has dispensed with the Aristotelian metaphysical framework that clings to self-identical essences and teleological causes, replacing it with a universe that has itself become dis-tracted in the sense of "diffused" or "dispersed", i.e. caught up in becoming, flux and differentiation. Having done away with both the concepts of *Heilsgeschichte* and the myth of universal progress and having severely problematized both our belief in the future and our faith in a restoration of the past, modern life can no longer be captured in meaningful forms and stable identities and of nothing it can truly be said that it has a *standpoint*, i.e. that it is located at its designated place. However, conjoining the flux of life with a reception in distraction, combining the heteronomy of the art-work with the autonomy of the aesthetic experience, art trains us to confront that change and it helps us to remain open to what is inherently non-anticipatable: distraction, hence, learns us that a universe that has lost its causes need not therefore itself be a lost cause.

This explains why the experience of seeing Van Gogh's paintings with his own eyes brought Captain Beefheart to exclaim that he was "disappointed in the sun". Rather than having to do with a feeling that the sun suddenly showed up someplace where he had not expected her to be, Beefheart was disappointed precisely on account of the feeling that she didn't, i.e. that, after having watched how Van Gogh managed to disperse and distract sunlight into a thousand tiny brushstrokes that make up cornfields, olive-trees, sunflowers or hay-stacks, upon exiting the museum it turned out that the real sun had kept herself still and immobile, having retained her steady place high above in the sky where Beefheart had last seen her when he entered the museum a couple of

[16] Walter Benjamin, "The Work of Art in the Age of Its Technological Reproducibility," 267.

hours earlier. Beefheart was disappointed that the sun had kept so still in one fixed spot because Van Gogh's pansolistic universe had shown him that she is in fact everywhere and that one need not even look at the sun in order to see her: for it is perfectly possible to see the sun even when one keeps one's back firmly turned to her, just like this farmer looks away from the setting sun yet discovers her refracted light everywhere in his surroundings, dis-tracting and diffusing (*verstreuen*) the seeds he's sowing, dispersing the life already contained in them to a field where nothing has a designated spot and where all that matters is to keep moving and to cover as much ground as one possibly can.

References

01. Benjamin, Walter, "Das Kunstwerk im Zeitalter seiner technischen Reproduzierbarkeit, Erste Fassung," *Gesammelte Schriften*, Band I-2, Rolf Tiedemann and Herman Schweppenhäuser, Frankfurt am Main: Suhrkamp Verlag, 1991.

02. Benjamin, Walter, "On Some Motifs in Baudelaire," *Selected Writings*, Volume 4, 1938-1940, Howard Eiland and Michael W. Jennings, Cambridge and London: The Belknap Press of Harvard University Press, 2003.

03. Benjamin, Walter. "The Work of Art in the Age of Its Technological Reproducibility. Third Version" in *Selected Writings*, Volume 4, 1938-1940, Howard Eiland and Michael W. Jennings, Cambridge and London: The Belknap Press of Harvard University Press, 2003.

04. Freud, Sigmund, "The Neuro-Psychoses of Defence (I)," *The Standard Edition of the Complete Psychological Works of Sigmund Freud*, Volume 3, James Strachey, London: Hogarth, 1953-1974.

05. Hansen, Miriam Bratu, "Benjamin and Cinema: Not a One-Way Street," *Critical Inquiry* 25. 2 ("Angelus Novus": Perspectives on Walter Benjamin, 1999): 306-343.

06. Jankélévitch, Vladimir, *La Musique et l'ineffable*, Paris: Éditions du Seuil, 1983.

07. Walser, Robert, *The Tanners*, New York: New Directions, 2009.

08. Weber, Samuel, "Citability - Of Gesture," *Benjamin's –abilities*, Cambridge and London: Harvard University Press, 2008.

09. Worringer, Wilhelm, *Abstraction and Empathy: A Contribution to the Psychology of Style*, Chicago: Ivan R. Dee, 2007.

12

Visualisation through Poetry

Concept of Spirituality and God in *The Prophet*

Ms. Winnie Jagadamma Panicker
Christ University, India

Poetry is an art form that is literary in nature, but which sublimely involves the relation of words to visuals. This is in a way related to intrapersonal communication, where the reader relates the words to the visuals he is related to. This paper will shed light upon the concept of spirituality and God that is made use of in the poetic essay *The Prophet* of Kahlil Gibran.[1] The kind of visuals that the human mind relates itself to while glancing through words, which are commonly used and which when used in the context of poetry changes its meaning are looked through this paper. It has explored the kind of thoughts that the poet has expressed about spirituality and God and has also explored the extent to which the poet has used the concept 'God lies within us' through his work.

Poetry is art that is born by the use of words. The word is of Greek origin and its etymological meaning is "making." Rhythm, rhyme and reason go hand-in-hand when it comes to poetry. Though the language of poetry is the language of emotions, it is not devoid of rationality either.

Trying to define poetry is almost not possible. The literature on it is really vast. Most famous poets have written about it. For Alexander

[1] Kahlil Gibran, *The Prophet*, in *The Greatest Works of Kahlil Gibran*, Mumbai: Jaico Publishing House, 1998.

Pope, for example, the essence of it came from what "oft was thought but never so well expressed," for Wordsworth it was a matter of the "overflow of powerful feelings, emotions recollected in tranquillity,"[2] Coleridge was perhaps the most ambitious in asserting that in writing poetry the human mind imitates the divine mind in a god-like act of creation.

Poetry is the creation of meaningful beauty by means of words, which thus both create and express who or what we are. There are no limits as to the subject matter of poetry. Whatever our human hearts and minds can contemplate or brood over or entertain is fair game. It is a form of art that employs word and visuals in the form of imagination. It is a medium that involves the utilisation of both the print and visual medium, where in the visual medium is subtly merged with the psychology of thinking. Written words can be related to visuals by way of imagination.

The skill developed in interpreting, judging, responding to and using visual representations of reality is called visual literacy. One should learn to 'see' a piece of art work to appreciate it. Visualization works out of the grey area of human perception and cognition. So far it has not been found to be self-consistent; there are no rules which precisely govern what approach will work under a given set of conditions. Visualization is not strictly repeatable; one user may perceive a relationship that may or may not be verifiable using visualization techniques while another sees nothing at all or something entirely different. Visualization relies on subjective interpretation; contextual cues are usually derived from "common" experience which is neither guaranteed to be common or commonly integrated into personal experience. Visualization is part of a process of discovery. It appears to aid the intuition in identifying relationships.

The essence of spirituality is the search to know our true selves, to discover the real nature of consciousness. This quest has been the foundation of all the great spiritual teachings, and the goal of all the great mystics.

---

[2] William Wordsworth, *Preface to The Lyrical Ballads*, India: Macmillan Publishers, 1981.

This paper has explored *The Prophet* by Kahlil Gibran. To give a few examples, let us take few lines from the poem.

> Almustafa, the chosen and the beloved, who was a dawn onto his own day, had waited twelve years in the city of Orphalese for his ship that was to return and bear him back to the isle of his birth.
> And in the twelfth year, on the seventh day of Ielool, the month of reaping, he climbed the hill without the city walls and looked seaward; and he beheld the ship coming with the mist.
> Then the gates of his heart were flung open, and his joy flew far over the sea. And he closed his eyes and prayed in the silences of his soul.[3]

These lines are taken from *The Prophet*. It talks about the feeling of Al Mustafa who had been waiting in the city of Orphalese for his ship that was to return and bear him back to the isle of his birth. In the second line, the writer mentions 'closed his eyes and prayed in the silences of his soul'. This single line has the interplay of four words that are closely related to spirituality which are eyes, prayer, silence and soul. The poet refers to the fact that one can find peace in himself by searching for God within oneself.

Philosopher *Lao Tzu* has said that 'Silence is a source of great strength'. Silence in the literal sense means the absence of sound or noise or a sense of absolute stillness. In a situation where there is a lot of noise around, one may not be able to find one's own self. Noise may be in different forms. It may not just be physical noise. Psychological noise is of great concern when trying to be in solitude. Psychological noise occurs when there is a blockage in the thought process or a disruption in the normal way a person thinks. When one seeks silence within oneself, then it is opening the pathway to find the soul within you.

In the lines of Kahlil Gibran where he says that the protagonist closed his eyes, then it refers to shutting his vision from the outside world and moving into a state of darkness from the physical world. One

[3] Kahlil Gibran, *The Prophet*, 1.

has to keep in mind the fact that closing ones eye will only shut him from the physical world. The entire world of imagination is still open to him. When one isolates himself from the outside world, then he seeks silence, with images from the past and experiences filling up to form images of spirituality within oneself. This stance when one begins to travel to the silence of his soul through the medium of prayer is mentioned in the above mentioned lines of Kahlil Gibran.

Mahatma Gandhi said "In the attitude of silence the soul finds the path in a clearer light, and what is elusive and deceptive resolves itself into crystal clearness. Our life is a long and arduous quest after truth."[4] Through these lines, the poet also reflects the thought that God lies within oneself and hence one prays to the silences of his soul.

These lines have a strong sense of visualisation. It is more of a direct way of visualising the words mentioned in the poem. In these line, "he climbed the hill without the city walls and looked seaward; and he beheld the ship coming with the mist", the reader can visualise the hill, a sea and the mist that covers a ship which is coming towards the protagonist. In the lines "Then the gates of his heart were flung open, and his joy flew far over the sea", the reader does visualise a human heart flinging open, but an image of a huge gate flinging open in front of the sea can be visualised. The lines "And he closed his eyes and prayed in the silences of his soul", employs more of an immaterial visualisation where a divine feel of the prayer and enlightenment is felt.

> And you, vast sea, sleeping mother,
> Who alone are peace and freedom to the river and the stream,
> Only another widening will this stream make, only another murmur in this glade,
> And then I shall come to you, a boundless drop to a boundless ocean.[5]

---

[4] "Mahatma Gandhi." Quotes.net. STANDS4 LLC, 22 Oct. 2012. http://www.quotes.net/ quote/34728.

[5] Kahlil Gibran, *The Prophet*, 3.

Here the poet talks about the existence of mankind and the ultimate destination of any living being on earth. The sea is referred to as the place for peace and freedom to the river and the stream. It means that the river and stream that is at one point of time bound by tangles and separated from its mother, will ultimately find its freedom when it reaches its mother, that is, the sea. The moment a human being is born, his life is destined to be degenerated in the soil. The various processes that the person goes through in a life changes the way every person lives. But, ultimately, in the end, every man reaches the end of life. The poet says, "[...] and then I shall come to you, a boundless drop to a boundless ocean."[6] This line refers to the same point. One can also come up with the meaning that the end of life means the attainment of eternity, which means spirituality. Here, a boundless ocean may also refer to the ocean of knowledge where the protagonist assures that he will go to. Ocean can be seen as a metaphor that is used to refer the vast and infinite world of knowledge and power and the pathway to attain spirituality. The Bible says "But memory-knowledge is signified by the sea in accordance with the density and blackness of its waters; and on the other hand, in accordance with their tenacity and transparency. From this it is that the memory-knowledge which looks to heaven, which is spiritual in the natural man, is called a glassy sea (Rev. 15:1, 2). That there shall be no reasoning about the truths of faith from memory-knowledges; but that truths shall be impressed on the heart, is signified by, the sea shall be no more" (Rev. 21:1). This substantiates the point that knowledge exists and truth will remain truth and there can be no reasoning for truth.

> A voice cannot carry the tongue and the lips that give it wings.
> Alone must it seek the ether.
> And alone and without his nest shall the eagle fly across the sun.
> Now when he reached the foot of the hill, he turned again towards the sea, and he saw his ship approaching the harbour, and upon her prow the mariners, the men of his own land.
> And his soul cried out to them, and he said:
> Sons of my ancient mother, you riders of the tides,

[6] Kahlil Gibran, *The Prophet*, 3

> How often have you sailed in my dreams. And now you come
> in my awakening, which is my deeper dream.
> Ready am I to go, and my eagerness with sails full set awaits
> the wind.[7]

These lines in a way explain that when one has to seek eternity, he would seek it alone and cannot take along with him any of the material things that he was associated with once. Just like how the voice that was totally dependent on the tongue and lips does not exist in reality with them. It is a medium that is created due to the working of the tongue and lips. The poet has related voice and the human self. One cannot depend on any material causes to attain eternity. This is explained in "Alone must it seek the ether". The ultimate aim of life is to realise the self. Once the self is attained then the person is alone.

There are various types of aloneness. *Kaivalya*, which is aloneness, is not a psychological aloneness. It is not a loneliness that is felt by the mind attached to this body. It is the loneliness of the spirit that is within us. Our soul is alone by itself. That we are, truly speaking, alone in this world is something very easy to understand. All the associations that we are speaking of - money, power, and social relations - are conditions artificially created by the coming together of a certain favourable atmosphere, because when a person is born as a little child, that child is totally alone to itself. It has no property; it has no consciousness of relations. It cannot know that it belongs to anybody, or anyone belongs to it.

This is what the poet is trying to explain through the lines "A voice cannot carry the tongue and the lips that gave it wings. Alone must it seek the ether." The spiritual thought in it is that one is alone while attaining spirituality. These verses have more of direct visualisation. In the line "And alone and without his nest shall the eagle fly across the sun", the reader is able to visualise an eagle, a horizon and a sun. When the poet says he saw his ship approaching the harbour, one can visualise a real ship approaching the harbour. However, one can think of immaterial visualisation where the reader can infer that the destiny of the protagonist was approaching him.

---

[7] Kahlil Gibran, *The Prophet*, 2-3.

Kahlil Gibran is a poet, author, philosopher who has written on the lines of spirituality and self realisation to a large extent. In the work *The Prophet*, he has constantly focussed on self realisation, attainment of spirituality and realising that God lies within one. Gibran used a strong array of words that emphasised on spirituality and the various aspects that are related to spirituality. All the concepts that the poet wanted to convey was conveyed successfully with the use of proper metaphors and symbols.

The Prophet is a journey from birth to death in a man's life. Whatever happens between birth and death and the various meanings that Gibran associated to them form the crux of the book. Gibran has strongly used visuals of spiritualisation in his book. There is a constant touch of spirituality in his works. The book proves that Gibran never gave out atheist thoughts on anything. The concept, 'God lies within us,' is being expressed in more than two areas in the book.

A strong influence of Eastern philosophy is seen in his works. Many stances of Biblical thoughts are also reflected in *The Prophet*. This is expressed in the line where the poet differentiates good and evil where he says that he could explain only good and not about one's evil. Evil is expressed as the absence of goodness.[8] The idea that the negative nature in human being should move away to reflect the positive in the human is also said in the Bible. This view is strongly expressed in the part where he explains about good and evil.

Born a Christian, Gibran also reflected thoughts on Sufism in his works. In the words of the Darqawi Sufi teacher Ahmad Ibn Ajiba, Sufism is "a science through which one can know how to travel into the presence of the Divine, purify one's inner self from filth, and beautify it with a variety of praiseworthy traits."[9] This is all reflected where Gibran speaks about knowing your inner self and realise the ultimate truth. Sufism is not selfishness, but altruism, kindness, affection, and service. It is not nonsense and idle talk but rather sincerity and wisdom. It produces purity in the heart, high knowledge and good works.

---

[8] Evil as '*privatio boni'* (privation of good) is one of the themes in the classical theodicy.

[9] *The Autobiography (Fahrasa) of a Moroccan Soufi: Ahmad ibn 'Ajiba*, trans. Jean-Louis Michon and David Streight, Louisville KY USA: Fons Vitae, 1999.

Therefore, Gibran has used the traits of Christianity, philosophy and Islamic philosophy in *The Prophet*. The researcher has reached the conclusion that the poet, Kahlil Gibran, has used the concept of 'spirituality' to express, in broad terms, that goodness and doing good deeds to humankind through the understanding and realisation of the self is the very value of our existence on the earth.

13

Contributors

Rev. Jose Panthaplamthottiyil is the Prior General of the CMI Congregation, and the Vice Chancellor of Dharmaram Vidya Kshetram, the Pontifical Athenaeum, Bangalore, India. He obtained his M.A. in International Studies from the University of Notre Dame, Indiana; M.S. in Journalism from the University of Illinois, and carried out his PhD Research in Mass Communications at Marquette University, Milwaukee, USA. His working experience spans from being a Lecturer at Christ College; HoD, Department of Journalism, Christ College; Visiting Lecturer, MG University; Chief-Editor of Deepika Daily and its Allied Publications; and Coordinator General of the CMI Congregation, Brooklyn, USA. He has to his credit several publications, including nine books in Malayalam, three books in Hindi and one book in English.

Dr. Alexandra Pleshoyano is an Associate Professor at the Faculty of Theology and Religious Studies at the University of Sherbrooke, and a Fellow at the Etty Hillesum Centre in Ghent, Belgium. After having obtained her PhD from the Radboud University in Nijmegen, the Netherlands, she carried out post-doctoral research at the University of Montreal, Canada, on *Metamorphosis of Leonard Cohen's Religious Figures*, and at the Katholieke Universiteit Leuven in Belgium, on *Etty Hillesum and Leonard Cohen.* She is the author of *J'avais encore mille choses à te demander. L'univers intérieur d'Etty Hillesum,* (2009) and *Etty Hillesum: l'amour comme* "seule solution". *Une herméneutique théologique au cœur du mal*, Münster (2007).

Dr. Ignatius Bambang Sugiharto is a Professor of Philosophy at the Philosophy Department, Parahyangan Catholic University, Bendung, Indonesia. He has served as the General Secretary of International Society for Universal Dialogue (2005-07); and President of Asian Association of Christian Philosophers (2006-08). He is a member of the Association of Philosophy Indonesia (ASAFI); and author of several books on Postmodernism, Contemporary Art, Culture, and Religions, including *Culture and Postmodern Philosophy* (1998), and *Culture and Cosmopolitanism* (2006).

Dr. Colby Dickinson is an Assistant Professor of Theology at Loyola University, Chicago. He holds a Master's Degree in Theological Studies (M.T.S.) from the Duke University (2000) and another in Master of Arts, Theology, Religious Education (M.A.) from Saint Louis University (2005) and PhD from the Katholieke Universiteit Leuven (2012). He is the author of *Agamben and Theology* (London, 2011), *Between the Canon and the Messiah: The Structure of Faith in Contemporary Continental Thought* (London, 2013) and Editor of *The Postmodern 'Saints' of France* (London, 2013) as well as a number of articles on Walter Benjamin, Jacques Derrida, Giorgio Agamben and Paul Ricoeur.

Ms. Elisabeth Bayley is a doctoral student at the Katholieke Universiteit Leuven, Belgium, where she is part of the research group 'Literary Studies: Literary Relations and Post/National Identities'. She holds a Master's Degree in Theology from the Aquinas Institute of Theology (2007) and Master of Arts, Literary Studies from the Katholieke Universiteit Leuven (2008). Her thesis is entitled "An Exploration of the Lie: Edith Wharton and Willa Cather's Deconstruction of Social Contracts and an Entrance into the Spiritual" where she is using theorists René Girard and Jacques Lacan to explore the ways in which lying functions within the works of Wharton and Cather, in order to maintain notions of a 'norm' within a society.

Dr. Jayanthi Kalpally Puthiyaveetil is a Consultant in the training division of Wipro Technologies, an IT company based in Bangalore,

India. She is a Certified Professional Behavioural Analyst and Basic Practionioner of Neuro-Linguistic Programming. As a trainer for the Middle Managers in her organization, she has trained people in the areas of Business Communication, Business Writing, Accent neutralization and Presentation Skills. An academic and researcher at heart, Jayanthi has worked in various academic institutions in India as a teacher of English. She has a Doctorate in English and her doctoral thesis is entitled "The Polyphonic Historical/ Narrative Voices in North American Native Women Writing." Her areas of interest include Tribal Literature, Native American Religions, Commonwealth Literature, Post-colonial Literature and Philosophy.

Dr. Marlies de Munck is a Research Fellow at the Institute of Philosophy, K.U. Leuven, Belgium. In 2007 she obtained her MPhil at the Institute of Philosophy, KUL, with a thesis on Susanne K. Langer's account of music and emotions. During the Fall of 2009-10 she was a Fulbright Visiting Scholar at the Philosophy Department of Columbia University, New York, USA. Recently she obtained her PhD with a dissertation about the construction of meaning in modern musical practices. Her fields of research encompass philosophical aesthetics, modernity critique and the philosophy of meaning, with a specific focus on music, literature and film. She has published several articles and contributed to a number of specialised volumes in aesthetics. Currently she is working on a new project about 'erosion and loss of meaning'.

Dr. Sanchita Choudhury is an Assistant Professor and DIC (Department in-charge) in Padmanava College of Engineering, Rourkela, in the Department of Humanities. She has completed her PhD from IIT Kharagpur in the field of Ethnomusicology. As a research scholar at IIT Kharagpur, she prepared this paper under the guidance of Professor Anjali Gera Roy, Dept. of Humanities and Social Sciences, IIT Kharagpur. Dr. Choudhury is also a performing artist (vocal). She is a poetry lover and spends time writing poems and experimenting with different genres of poetry. She is a UGC trainer of Capacity Building of Women Managers. Her research interests include Cultural Studies, Cultural Theory, Environmental Studies, Ethnomusicology, Feminist Theology, and Musicology.

Dr. Sebastian Elavathingal is a Professor of Missiology and Aesthetics. He studied the cultural aspect of Christian Mission in India and took Doctorate in Missiology from the Gregorian University, Rome. He is an Alumnus of the Brera Fine Arts Academy, Milan (1991-1995). He has served as the Rector of Samanvaya Theological College, Bhopal, India (2005-2011), and the Editor of the Journal of Spirituality, *In Christo*. He is the author of many articles on art and theology and presented papers on art, communication and spirituality at the national and international conferences. He has published the research work under the title, *Inculturation and Christian Art: An Indian Perspective* (Rome: Urbanian University Press, 1990).

Dr. Stéphane Symons is an Assistant Professor at the Centre for Metaphysics and Philosophy of Culture, Institute of Philosophy, K.U. Leuven, Belgium. His doctoral dissertation was on Walter Benjamin "Traces of Truth, Images of Hope." He has contributed a chapter "Walter Benjamin" in: P. Livingston and C. Plantinga, eds., *The Routledge Companion to Philosophy and Film* (London, 2009). He has published several scientific articles on twentieth century continental philosophy of art and aesthetics, mainly in French and German. He also serves as a member of the Council of the Institute of Philosophy, and a member of the Contemporary Art Committee.

Ms. Winnie Jagadamma Panicker is a Post Graduate in Mass Communication and a Graduate in Videography and Mass Communication. She worked in "Kerala Calling Magazine" as translator, content editor and writer; as content writer for "Kerala Handbook" (2010) published by the Government of Kerala; and as Production Coordinator for the documentary, funded by Bill & Melinda Gates, named "Reclaiming Paradise." Ms. Panicker served as a Guest Lecturer at Mar Ivanios College, Thiruvananthapuram. She has published two books of poems: *Loveliness of Dawn* (Malu Ben Publishers, 2004) and *Flowers on the Violin* (Blue Mango Books, 2009).

14

Index of Names

15

Index of Themes